NEW YORK CITY

Like a
Local

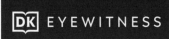

NEW YORK CITY
Like a Local

BY THE PEOPLE WHO CALL IT HOME

Contents

EAT

DRINK

SHOP

ARTS & CULTURE

meet the locals

LAUREN PALEY

Born and raised just outside of NYC, Lauren has lived in Morocco, France, and Southeast Asia, but it's the East Village that she calls home these days. Marketer by day, writer by night, Lauren is constantly on the hunt for Thai food joints, cozy wine bars, and quirky indie bookstores.

BRYAN PIROLLI

Bryan has been off-and-on with NYC since 2004, calling it home when not in Paris. It was at NYU that Bryan began his journalism career. Now a teacher, he is also a devotee of the New York Road Runners and Front Runners and spends hours jogging Prospect Park, not to mention chasing down Chinese food.

KWEKU ULZEN

Having moved from Toronto to the Deep South and then to NYC, Kweku settled in Crown Heights, Brooklyn. He's kept busy as a software engineer but finds time to volunteer with high school kids and political organizations. Kweku unwinds by playing basketball and hosting wine-fueled dinner parties.

NIGHTLIFE

OUTDOORS

New York City

WELCOME TO THE CITY

New Yorkers are as diverse as the city itself – a patchwork of ages, nationalities, ethnicities, and personalities that make up this exhilarating metropolis. The cab driver who speeds through yellow lights with abandon, the young artist pinning her hopes on a fresh start in the city, the withered man who's been sipping coffee at his local diner for more than a decade. But, as varied as they are, it's easy to spot a New Yorker: they're resilient, savvy, and passionately proud of their city. (And all claim to know the best pizza spot in town.)

Living in NYC requires grit: navigating the crush of the subway, enduring the cacophony of taxis honking at 3am, rebuilding a downtown forever devoid of the Twin Towers. Locals often complain about the city like it's their unruly problem child. Yet they still love it, because beyond the noise, dirt, and hardship, there's something magical about New York City. And it's this something that keeps visitors returning time after time.

Of course, glimpsing the city's iconic skyline is thrilling. But those glitzy steel structures are just a fraction of the city's character. NYC is also squat tenements criss-crossed by rusty fire escapes, and school yards emblazoned with graffiti. It's everything at once: history and high-rises, nature and urbanism, shabby and chic.

New York City can be chaotic and overwhelming. But that's where this book comes in. We know the places New Yorkers love best, from the rooftop bars they'll wait all week for, to the art galleries based in people's apartments. In a city of more than 8 million, it's impossible to capture everyone's experience. Rather, this book celebrates snapshots of life in a city that's as diverse as its locals.

Whether you're a New Yorker looking to rediscover your city, or you're a visitor wanting to rip up the traditional "to do" list, this book will help you embrace a lesser-known New York City. Enjoy NYC, but do it the local way.

Liked by the locals

"New York has this irresistible, frenetic energy that I love. The simple act of walking around – inhaling the scent of cheap pizza alongside haute cuisine, soaking in the never-ending stream of people – is the most invigorating feeling. It's like being at the center of the universe."

LAUREN PALEY, MARKETING MANAGER
AND TRAVEL WRITER

There's no off-season in New York – something is always afoot in the city. Think jolly parades in spring, alfresco shows in summer, and festive fun in winter.

New York City
THROUGH THE YEAR

SPRING

THE GREAT OUTDOORS
Surviving the brittle New York winters makes spring that much sweeter for locals. Windows are flung open, bulky layers are shed, and long walks are relished in the newfound warmth.

STREET FOOD MARKETS
Food vendors tempt hungry New Yorkers out of their apartments at the likes of Brooklyn's Smorgasburg, Midtown's Broadway Bites, and the International Night Market in Queens *(p47)*.

PARADING IN THE STREET
New Yorkers *love* to remind others that they're part-Irish, so naturally the St. Patrick's Day Parade is a jubilant family affair. Not far behind is a sea of flower-bedecked bonnets at the Easter Parade on Easter Sunday.

BASEBALL SEASON
Sports fanatics flock to the city's stadiums to welcome six months of baseball – and root for the New York Yankees, of course.

SUMMER

PARK PICNICS
Locals stock up on artisanal treats and bottles of wine at farmers' markets and relish lazy afternoon park get-togethers.

OUTDOOR MOVIE THEATERS
Screens pop up across NYC, fronted by deck chairs and featuring an enviable backdrop: the sparkling city skyline.

LIVE EVENTS

Parks host outdoor events in summertime, like show-stopping Broadway previews in Bryant Park and Shakespeare's greatest hits in Central Park.

ALFRESCO DINING

New York becomes electric during the summer, with the energy buzzing around its outdoor dining scene. Patios overflow with groups and restaurants get creative with alfresco seating.

FALL

THE PUMPKIN CRAZE

Come fall, nearly every coffee shop and bakery adds pumpkin into their menu: pumpkin lattes, donuts, even craft beers.

FALL FOLIAGE

Weekends are reserved for long walks to soak in the fiery auburn hues of the season. Central Park is a favorite spot, though many escape upstate for a day of fall foliage and apple picking.

HALLOWEEN HAPPENINGS

Spooky decor and costume parties take over the city in October, with the fun culminating at the Village Halloween Parade. The city's furry friends can also be seen in cute outfits at the Tompkins Square Halloween Dog Parade.

GIVING THANKS

Families unite to watch giant balloons float along the city streets for the Macy's Thanksgiving Day Parade before they tuck into turkey and all the trimmings.

WINTER

FAIRY TALE IN NEW YORK

The movies don't lie: nowhere does Christmas like the Big Apple. Lights are draped everywhere, department stores compete for attention with their dazzling window displays, and locals take to the Rockefeller and Central Park ice rinks.

COZY INDOORS

When snow starts to settle (and, boy, does it settle), locals head inside and enjoy dinner parties, bottles of red in a snug wine bar, or movie nights in their PJs.

THE BALL DROP

Sure, some locals take to Times Square to welcome in the year with the famous ball drop, but most are home with their loved ones and a fridge full of drinks.

There's an art to being a New Yorker, from the dos and don'ts of eating out to negotiating the city's hectic streets. Here's a breakdown of all you need to know.

New York City
KNOW-HOW

For a directory of health and safety resources, safe spaces, and accessibility information, turn to page 190. For everything else, read on.

EAT
Brunch is a weekend institution in NYC and restaurants start filling up from 11am. During the week, New Yorkers rarely head straight home after work – they love to eat dinner out, around 7 or 8pm. Reservations are a must, though many spots are first-come, first-serve, so put your name down and grab a drink elsewhere. Note that waitstaff are pretty forthright and may ask you to leave once the meal is over (don't be offended).

DRINK
Coffee fuels New York, and working cafés are a huge part of daily life. That said, more and more coffee shops are going wifi- and laptop-free so, if you're hoping to connect to the internet, check with a barista before you order.

Evening drinks can be expensive but the city is a big fan of happy hour deals, which are generally offered from 5pm. After an upscale drinking den? Reservations are a good idea for wine and cocktail bars. In general, if there's a hostess who seats you, someone will also take your order at the table; at more casual spots, just head straight to the bar.

SHOP
Stores are usually open seven days a week but with reduced hours on Sundays. Sales associates are generally helpful and friendly, so don't be surprised if they start doling out advice and coaxing you toward a fitting room. Oh, and carry a tote to avoid a paper bag charge (plastic bags are outlawed).

ARTS & CULTURE

New York's museums and galleries aren't cheap to enter, costing $15–30. Some cultural establishments do offer pay-as-you-wish at the door, but the line can be long, which is when booking ahead of time is sensible. Broadway is also incredibly expensive, with a decent seat costing $100–300, so New Yorkers prefer more thrifty off-Broadway performances. The scene is very casual these days, so there's no need to dress up.

NIGHTLIFE

New York isn't a cheap city, so nights out tend to start in a dive bar or with a happy hour deal. It's also the city that never sleeps, remember, so pace yourself. Comedy shows begin early, around 7:30pm, and there's usually a two-drink minimum on top of each ticket. Clubs and live music venues start to fill up around 10 or 11pm, with long lines forming after that, and include a cover charge. When it comes to what to wear, anything goes – dress up or down, whatever you wish. Just be sure to have your ID on you, as carding is rampant.

OUTDOORS

When the sun shines, New Yorkers love to picnic and barbecue in the city's parks. Sadly, littering is an issue in the city so avoid adding to the problem and take your garbage with you. There's also a big homeless population in New York City, so it's not uncommon to be approached for food in outdoor spaces.

Keep in mind

Here are some more tips and tidbits that will help you fit in like a local.

» **Keep cash handy** Much of the city is cashless but some smaller establishments remain cash-only, so it's best to have both a card and dollars to hand.

» **No smoking** Smoking is strictly prohibited inside. If you have to light up, do it outside.

» **Always tip** Adding at least 15, if not 20, percent to your bill is a must at restaurants, bars, sit-down cafés, and in taxis.

» **Stay hydrated** Plenty of cafés and restaurants are happy to refill your reusable water bottle – just ask nicely.

GETTING AROUND

New York City is made up of five boroughs: Manhattan, the Bronx, Queens, Brooklyn, and Staten Island. To the west of Manhattan is the Hudson River, to the east is – wait for it – the East River, and the two meet in New York Harbor. Much of Manhattan is organized in an easy-to-navigate grid system, with streets divided into east and west, and street numbers climbing as you head north. That said, Lower Manhattan and the rest of the boroughs aren't as neatly organized.

To keep things simple we've provided what3words addresses for each sight in this book, meaning you can quickly pinpoint exactly where you're heading.

On foot

It might be a sprawling metropolis, but NYC is best explored on foot; you'll be helping the environment and get to see the city in all its glory, too. The grid system in Manhattan helps work out how many blocks you need to walk to get from A to B, though bear in mind that there are a lot of traffic lights (and the occasional bottleneck of people), which will slow you down a bit. New Yorkers walk with purpose – in other words, very quickly – so don't be alarmed if fast walkers bypass you. If you do need to stop and check a what3words location, step to the inside of the sidewalk.

On wheels

Biking is a really popular way to get around but it's not for the faint of heart. The city's bike lanes get congested and you need to be aware of things like jaywalking pedestrians, cars making left turns, and the city's famously aggressive motorists. Our top tip? Stick to one side of the bike lane so other bikers can pass you (seriously, they'll love you for it). This is the only time we'll advise you not to do as the locals do: follow the flow of traffic to guarantee everyone's safety (even if you see other cyclists doing otherwise) and always wear a helmet.

The city's official bikeshare program, CitiBike, offers bikes to rent from one of its 950 docking stations for one ride ($3) or 24 hours ($15). If you're after a casual pedal around Central Park, you can rent a lightweight bike from Bike Rental Central Park. Though it's more expensive than CitiBike (1 hour is $9, 2 hours $14, 4 hours $19), it's totally worth it; bikes come with a helmet and padlock for added security (and peace of mind). *www.citibikenyc.com*
www.bikerentalcentralpark.com

By public transportation

The Metropolitan Transportation Authority (MTA) looks after the city's public transportation network, which runs 24/7. The subway system is easy to to navigate once you're clear on whether you want to travel uptown or downtown (remember the grid system). When entering or exiting a subway station, be sure to stand right, walk left – the locals will genuinely appreciate this. Alternatively, the city's bus system is another easy way of getting around.

The easiest way to pay for either the bus or the subway is with a MetroCard, which you can buy from any MTA kiosk. One journey, or one swipe of the paper MetroCard, costs $2.75, or you can buy a 7-day MetroCard for $33 and take as many journeys as you like. Note that buses only accept exact change for a journey, so a MetroCard really is a must-buy.

By car or taxi

No one (except Staten Islanders) owns a car in New York City. Instead, New Yorkers use those iconic yellow cabs, though the traffic-clogged streets mean public transportation is often a better choice, even in rush hour. Outside of Manhattan, locals largely rely on taxi apps like Uber and Lyft.

Download these

We recommend you download these apps to help you get about the city.

WHAT3WORDS
Your geocoding friend
A what3words address is a simple way to communicate any precise location on earth, using just three words. ///frog.thin.above, for example, is the code for the John Lennon memorial. Simply download the free what3words app, type a what3words address into the search bar, and you'll know exactly where to go.

MTA
Your local transportation service
The MyMTA app lays out all your best options for moving around the city, as well as live departures, service changes, and delay information for each stop.

*New York City is a vast mosaic of neighborhoods,
each patch with its own character and community.
Here we take a look at some of our favorites.*

New York City
NEIGHBORHOODS

Alphabet City

Fast-gentrifying but still genuinely multicultural, with strong Hispanic and Jewish communities, this enclave is a hipster haven thanks to its grungy dive bars and cool cocktail joints. {map 2}

Bed-Stuy

Brooklyn outpost Bed-Stuy has known difficult times: it suffered in the Depression and then saw race riots in the 1960s. Today this bastion of Black culture is thriving, with small businesses popping up left, right, and center. {map 4}

Dumbo

Mercifully shortened from "Down Under the Manhattan Bridge Overpass," Dumbo epitomizes Brooklyn's creative character. Trendy and innovative, the area is awash with cool art spaces and start-ups housed in converted warehouses, plus foodie mecca TimeOut Market. {map 5}

East Village

Once the heart of the city's punk scene, the East Village is now the turf of young professionals who love the remnants of its grungy past. Weekends are spent combing the area's thrift stores for a bargain and reveling in its top-notch nightlife. {map 2}

Flatiron District

The clue's in the name: this is the home of the iconic Flatiron Building, which watches over workers hot-footing it to the office in this busy business hub. {map 1}

Greenpoint

Often called "Little Poland," Greenpoint has long been a Polish district but the Brooklyn 'hood has seen contentious gentrification recently, with organic food stores popping up next to old-school pierogi joints. {map 4}

Greenwich Village

When the gay community demonstrated here in 1969, following a police raid, "the Village" became an LGBTQ+ landmark. Years after the Stonewall riots, people love this inclusive area for its live theater and comedy. {map 1}

Harlem

This hub of Black and Latin American culture is known for the Harlem Renaissance, which saw African American creative arts thrive in the 1920s. The artistic boom isn't just a thing of the past; fancy some live jazz? Harlem's got you. {map 3}

Hell's Kitchen

Favored by the LGBTQ+ community and actors from nearby Broadway, this patch promises a rip-roaring night out. Things kick off in one of the area's umpteen restaurants before a bar crawl through the 'hood. {map 3}

Lower East Side

This multiethnic neighbor-hood is a window to the past. The Tenement Museum reminds locals of the area's history of immigration, and Jewish heritage lives on in family-run delis. {map 2}

Meatpacking District

A gritty center for meat processing until the mid-20th century, this district now houses the city's priciest real estate. Luxury storefronts and an uber-cool bar scene attract a sophisticated, monied crowd looking to put down roots here. {map 1}

Nolita

Forget Little Italy. North of Little Italy – aka Nolita – is where it's at. Upscale shops and cute trattorias tucked down narrow streets attract well-dressed fashionistas for boutique browsing and leisurely lunches. {map 1}

Park Slope

Cool mamas and their strollers rule the sidewalks in Brooklyn's village-like Park Slope, where organic markets and mom-and-pop shops bump up against community bookstores. {map 5}

Prospect Heights

Prospect Heights showcases the best of Brooklyn. It's home to big-hitters like Brooklyn Museum and Prospect Park, but it's the incredible dining scene that locals can't get enough of. {map 5}

Red Hook

When New Yorkers want to escape the city, they head to Brooklyn's Red Hook. Here, cobblestone streets and shipping yards make a lovely backdrop to seafood shacks and breweries. {map 5}

Upper East Side

Beautiful townhouses and fancy restaurants have long attracted blue-blooded New Yorkers to this part of the city. But the Upper East Side isn't just for socialites; visitors flock here for the world-class Met, Frick, and Guggenheim. {map 3}

Upper West Side

Squeezed between Riverside Park and Central Park, this is one of the greenest, quietest areas; it's no wonder families aspire to live here. {map 3}

Williamsburg

Brooklyn's "Billyburg" is a study in contrasts: Hasidic Jews live side-by-side with hipsters, trendy roasteries occupy tattered warehouses, and old-world dance halls have been transformed into trendy clubs. {map 4}

New York City

ON THE MAP

Whether you're looking for your new favorite spot or want to check out what each part of New York City has to offer, our maps – along with handy map references throughout the book – have you covered.

NEWARK

MILLBURN

NEW JERSEY

ELIZABETH

CRANFORD

LINDEN

ELM PARK

PLAINFIELD

STATEN
ISLAND

WOODBRIDGE

METUCHEN

ELTINGVILLE

Lower
New York Bay

0 kilometers 5

0 miles 5

Hudson River

CHELSEA

MANHATTAN

MEATPACKING DISTRICT

WEST VILLAGE

GREENWICH VILLAGE

HUDSON SQUARE

SOHO

NOHO

NOLITA

TRIBECA

MANHATTAN

LITTLE ITALY

Le Bain **D**

The High Line **O**

The Whitney Museum of American Art **A**

Ninth Avenue **O**

A Ivy Brown Gallery

A The Rubin

Raines Law Room **D**

JACKSON SQUARE

WEST 14TH STREET

EIGHTH AVENUE

SEVENTH AVENUE

SIXTH AVENUE

WEST 19TH STREET

WEST 15TH STREET

Cubbyhole **N**

ABINGDON SQUARE

Magnolia Bakery **E**

WEST STREET

WASHINGTON STREET

WEST STREET

GREENWICH AVENUE

McCARTHY SQUARE

Julius' **D**

VILLAGE SQUARE

E Alta

E Aunt Jake's

WEST 12TH STREET

FIFTH AVENUE

UNIVERSITY PLACE

Employees Only **D**

Marie's Crisis **D**

Playhouse **N**

E Buvette

Grove Street **O**

Goods for the Study **S**

WEST 8TH ST

O MacDougal Alley

EAST 8TH STREET

The IFC Center **A**

Blue Note **N**

Village Underground **N**

E Tokyo Record Bar

Comedy Cellar

The Uncommons **N**

O Washington Square Park

GREENWICH VILLAGE

BROADWAY

The Public Theater

MORTON STREET

CLARKSON STREET

WEST HOUSTON STREET

Film Forum **A**

HUDSON SQUARE

HUDSON STREET

VARICK STREET

SIXTH AVENUE

WEST HOUSTON STREET

E The Dutch

Angelika Film Center **A**

Housing Works **S**

SPRING STREET

SOHO

Lafayette **E**

LAFAYETTE ST

NOHO

S Kith

Bowery Poetry Club

D Botanica **N**

Elizabeth Street **O**

A Bowery Mural

CANAL STREET

GREENWICH STREET

WEST STREET

MANHATTAN

Krewe **S**

BROOME STREET

GRAND STREET

CANAL STREET

L'Appartement Sézane **S**

McNally Jackson

Eileen's Special Cheesecake **E**

La Compagnie des Vins Surnaturels **D**

NOLITA

O

Elizabeth Street Garden

BROADWAY

TRIBECA

Soho Repertory Theatre **A**

FINN SQUARE

A Canada

LITTLE ITALY

BOWERY

CHRYSTIE STREET

ELIZABETH STREET

A Artists Space

0 meters 400
0 yards 400

MAP 1

🅔 EAT

ABCV (p40)
Alta (p42)
Aunt Jake's (p53)
Buvette (p55)
The Dutch (p40)
Eileen's Special
    Cheesecake (p51)
Lafayette (p42)
Magnolia Bakery (p51)
Tokyo Record Bar (p39)
Union Square Café (p43)

🅓 DRINK

Le Bain (p70)
Botanica (p76)
La Compagnie des
    Vins Surnaturels (p65)
Employees Only (p60)
Julius' (p79)
Marie's Crisis (p78)
Raines Law Room (p62)

🅢 SHOP

L'Appartement Sézane (p104)
Fishs Eddy (p103)
Goods for the Study (p102)
Housing Works (p93)
Kith (p106)
Krewe (p106)
McNally Jackson (p92)

🅐 ARTS & CULTURE

Angelika Film Center (p135)
Artists Space (p122)
Bowery Mural (p125)
Canada (p120)
Film Forum (p135)
The IFC Center (p132)
Ivy Brown Gallery (p121)
The Public Theater (p131)
The Rubin (p117)
Soho Repertory Theatre (p131)
The Whitney Museum of
    American Art (p119)

🅝 NIGHTLIFE

Blue Note (p151)
Bowery Poetry Club (p144)
Comedy Cellar (p142)
Cubbyhole (p161)
Playhouse (p162)
The Uncommons (p155)
Village Underground (p141)

🅞 OUTDOORS

Elizabeth Street (p183)
Elizabeth Street Garden (p177)
Grove Street (p180)
The High Line (p169)
MacDougal Alley (p181)
Ninth Avenue (p183)
Washington Square Park (p168)

MAP 2

2

Ⓔ EAT

Beauty & Essex *(p41)*
Clinton St. Baking Company *(p32)*
Essex Market *(p45)*
Ferns *(p53)*
Hotel Chantelle *(p34)*
Ippudo *(p37)*
Morgenstern's Finest Ice Cream *(p48)*
Petee's Pies *(p51)*
Russ & Daughters Cafe *(p33)*
Somtum Der *(p39)*
Van Leeuwen *(p49)*

Ⓓ DRINK

Abraço *(p81)*
Apotheke *(p61)*
Bibi Wine Bar *(p67)*
Black Cat LES *(p80)*
CloudM Rooftop Bar Bowery *(p71)*
Coffee Project NY *(p82)*
Garfunkel's *(p63)*
Fish Bar *(p76)*
McSorley's *(p75)*
Mr. Purple *(p71)*
Pouring Ribbons *(p62)*
Proletariat *(p72)*
Ruffian *(p67)*
Sake Bar Decibel *(p60)*

Ⓢ SHOP

A1 Records *(p97)*
Assembly New York *(p104)*
Coming Soon *(p101)*

Crystals Garden *(p100)*
Cure Thrift Shop *(p91)*
Mr. Throwback *(p90)*
Stranded Records *(p98)*

Ⓐ ARTS & CULTURE

First Street Green
Cultural Park *(p124)*
Freeman Alley *(p125)*
La MaMa Experimental
Theatre Club *(p129)*
Metrograph *(p133)*
Museum of the American Gangster *(p115)*
Museum of Reclaimed
Urban Space *(p114)*
New York Theatre Workshop *(p129)*
Tenement Museum *(p112)*
Village East Cinema *(p134)*

Ⓝ NIGHTLIFE

Ace Bar *(p152)*
Bowery Electric *(p148)*
Caveat *(p146)*
Dream Baby *(p156)*
Home Sweet Home *(p159)*
Nuyorican Poets Cafe *(p146)*
Rockwood Music Hall *(p151)*
Solas *(p157)*

Ⓞ OUTDOORS

6th Street and Avenue B
Community Garden *(p177)*
Liz Christy Community Garden *(p178)*

Book Culture **S** BROADWAY

SOUTH HARLEM

67 Orange Street **D**

Graffiti H of Far

El Museo del Barrio **A**
A

NEW JERSEY

North Hudson Park

GUTTENBERG

62ND STREET

WEST NEW YORK

PORT IMPERIAL BOULEVARD

RIVER ROAD

HENRY HUDSON PARKWAY

WEST 96TH ST

WEST 86TH ST

BROADWAY

AMSTERDAM AVENUE

COLUMBUS AVENUE

CENTRAL PARK WEST

Central Park

UPPER WEST SIDE

Museum of the City of New York **A**

EAST 96TH

Cooper Hewitt Smithsonian Design Museum **A**

Jacob's Pickles **E**

Westsider Rare and Used Books **S** WEST 81ST ST

Stand Up NY **N**

Levain Bakery **E**

Vin Sur Vingt **D**

American Museum of Natural History **A**

The New-York Historical Society **A**

N 92nd Street

DTUT

FIFTH AVENUE

MADISON AVENUE

PARK AVENUE

EAST 96TH ST

EAST 86TH ST

EAST 79TH ST

Hudson River

WEST 72ND ST

WEST 66TH ST

AMSTERDAM AVE

COLUMBUS AVE

CENTRAL PARK WEST

WEST 57TH ST

O Central Park

UPPER EAST SIDE

EAST 72ND ST

EAST 65TH ST

Roosevelt Island

HELL'S KITCHEN

MANHATTAN

N Dizzy's Club

N Hardware

Rudy's Bar & Grill **D**

Signature Theatre Company **A** WEST 42ND ST

Los Tacos No. 1 **E**

TWELFTH AVE

ELEVENTH AVE

TENTH AVENUE

NINTH AVENUE

EIGHTH AVENUE

SEVENTH AVENUE

SIXTH AVE

FIFTH AVE

The Paris Theater **A**

Rough Trade **S**

EAST 57TH ST

PARK AVENUE

THIRD AVENUE

SECOND AVENUE

FIRST AVENUE

ROOSEVELT DRIVE

FRANKLIN D ROOSEVELT DR

Kinokuniya **S**

The Tank **N**

Bryant Park **O**

Bookmarks **D**

MIDTOWN

EAST 42ND ST

Gallow Green **D**

Magnet Theater **N**

Patent Pending **D**

Jongro BBQ **E**

The Morgan Library & Museum **A**

CHELSEA

WEST 23RD ST

Barcade **N**

Gotham Comedy Club **N**

230 Fifth **D**

BROADWAY

The Old Print Shop **S**

PARK AVE SOUTH

EAST 23RD ST

East River

HUNTERS POINT

VERNON BLVD

11TH STREET

The Kitchen **A**

WEST 14TH ST

FIRST AVENUE

0 kilometers 1
0 miles 1

RIVER ROAD

MAP 3

E EAT

D DRINK

S SHOP

A ARTS & CULTURE

N NIGHTLIFE

O OUTDOORS

MAP 4

4

EXPRESSWAY

MASPETH

FLUSHING AVENUE

AVENUE

AVENUE

RIDGEWOOD

CYPRESS AVENUE

AVENUE

AVENUE

AVENUE

BROADWAY

E Le District

CIVIC CENTER

CANAL STREET

BOWERY

GRAND STREET

LOWER EAST SIDE

Williamsburg Bridge **O**

CHURCH STREET

BROADWAY

MANHATTAN

EAST BROADWAY

LOWER MANHATTAN

ROOSEVELT DRIVE

O Walk the East River Promenade

WEST STREET

BROADWAY

WATER ST

FRANKLIN D.

E Manhatta

Manhattan Bridge

East River

Brooklyn Bridge

O The Battery Urban Farm
O The Battery

O Ride the Staten Island Ferry

St. Ann's Warehouse **A** **E** TimeOut Market

DUMBO

A Dumbo Walls

Rollerblade along Brooklyn Bridge Park **O**

Brooklyn Bridge Park **O**

HENRY ST

FLUSHING AVENUE

Kayak the **O** East River

DOWNTOWN BROOKLYN

BROOKLYN

Brooklyn Historical Society **A**

MYRTLE AVENUE

VANDERBILT

Joralemon Street **O**

S Collyer's Mansion

GOVERNORS ISLAND

New York Transit Museum **A**

ATLANTIC AVE

BAM Harvey Theater **A**

Imani **E**

O Governors Island Teaching Garden

COLUMBIA STREET

BROOKLYN-QUEENS EXPRESSWAY

HENRY ST

E La Vara

BOERUM HILL

N Center for Fiction

FULTON ST

June **D**

SMITH ST

E Rucola

WYCKOFF STREET

Clover Club **N**

S Books Are Magic

N Gotham Archery

FLATBUSH

PROSPECT HEIGHTS

CARROLL GARDENS

Royal Palms Shuffleboard **N**

Littlefield **N**

Beacon's Closet **S**

VAN BRUNT STREET

A Amorphic Robot Works

N The Punderdome

Unnameable Books **S**

AVENUE

Red Hook Winery **D**

Canoe the **O** Gowanus Canal

UNION STREET

GRAND ARMY PLA

D Sunny's Bar

GOWANUS EXPRESSWAY

GOWANUS CANAL

E Al Di La Trattoria

3RD AVENUE

4TH AVENUE

3RD STREET

S Community Bookstore

RED HOOK

The Bell House **N**

Red Hook Park

S The Big Reuse

PARK SLOPE

9TH STREET

BROOKLYN

5TH AVENUE

7TH AVENUE

PROSPECT PARK WEST

O Prospect Park

0 kilometers   1

0 miles   1

MAP 5

0 kilometers 5
0 miles 5

Van Cortlandt Park **O**

EAST
BRONX

FORT
LEE

Tunnel Street **A**

WEST
BRONX

BRONX

MORRIS
PARK

NEW JERSEY

The Audubon Mural Project **A**

SOUTH
BRONX

Striver's Row **O**
Schomburg Center for
Research in Black Culture **O**

St. Nicholas Park **O**
The Studio Museum in Harlem **A** **O** **N**
N **O** La Finca del Sur **O**
O **S** The Lit. Bar **S**

Shrine
Harlem
Grown

SECAUCUS

UNION
CITY

Rocky McBride's **D**
S Belief **S**

MANHATTAN

ASTORIA

Mahmoud's **E**
E Corner

JACKSON
HEIGHTS

MURRAY
HILL

HOBOKEN

O
Brooklyn Grange **E** Amdo
Rooftop Farm **E** Kitchen

Queens International
Night Market **E**

CORONA

QUEENS

JERSEY
CITY

See maps 1–5
for Central New York

FOREST
HILLS

JAMAIC

RIDGEWOOD

Upper
New York
Bay

Nowadays **N**

OZONE
PARK

BROWNSVILLE

BROOKLYN

SUNSET
PARK

FLATBUSH

CANARSIE

ST.
GEORGE

Pacificana **E**

E The Farm
on Adderley

BAY
RIDGE

MIDWOOD

STATEN
ISLAND

GRAVESEND

SHEEPSHEAD
BAY

Lower
New York
Bay

CONEY ISLAND

Coney Island **D**
Brewery

O Relax on
Brighton Beach

ROCKAWAY
PARK

MAP 6

E EAT

Amdo Kitchen *(p44)*

The Farm on Adderley *(p32)*

Mahmoud's Corner *(p46)*

Pacificana *(p39)*

Queens International
Night Market *(p47)*

D DRINK

Coney Island Brewery *(p75)*

Rocky McBride's *(p77)*

S SHOP

Belief *(p107)*

The Lit. Bar *(p93)*

A ARTS & CULTURE

The Audubon Mural Project *(p126)*

The Studio Museum in
Harlem *(p122)*

Tunnel Street *(p126)*

N NIGHTLIFE

Nowadays *(p158)*

Schomburg Center for Research
in Black Culture *(p146)*

Shrine *(p158)*

O OUTDOORS

Brooklyn Grange Rooftop
Farm *(p178)*

Harlem Grown *(p179)*

La Finca del Sur *(p176)*

Relax on Brighton Beach *(p175)*

St. Nicholas Park *(p171)*

Striver's Row *(p182)*

Van Cortlandt Park *(p170)*

GREAT
NECK

BAYSIDE

QUEENS
VILLAGE

ST.
ALBANS

ROSEDALE

FAR
ROCKAWAY

EAT

Savor handmade pasta in cozy digs, devour food-truck dumplings, or nab melt-in-the-middle cookies to go – NYC supplies endless culinary delights, no matter your mood.

Brunch Spots

Is there a meal more New York than brunch?
Fluffy pancakes, doughy bagels, homely diner fare –
brunch not only ritualizes the weekend but it
celebrates the city's wonderfully diverse food scene.

THE FARM ON ADDERLEY

Map 6; 1108 Cortelyou Road, Flatbush, Brooklyn;
///scars.tinsel.vines; www.thefarmonadderley.com

Brunch has never tasted so worthy. It's all about supporting local
suppliers and plating up classic brunch fare with seasonal ingredients
at this farm-to-table restaurant. And if the sustainable mission
statement isn't enough to woo you, there's also a verdant back patio
decorated with rickety wooden furniture and walls of greenery –
ideal for warm-weather brunching alongside laid-back Brooklynites.

CLINTON ST. BAKING COMPANY

Map 2; 4 Clinton Street, Lower East Side; ///anyway.output.closet;
www.clintonstreetbaking.com

You know a place is special when there's a line of hopefuls waiting
patiently outside. Mom-and-pop bakery Clinton St. is a local icon
thanks to its fluffy-beyond-compare pancakes. Inside, the energy is

The wait can last for two hours so put your name down early and wait with a coffee at Black Cat LES *(p80)*.

frenetic: pans clang, servers run and zigzag like quarterbacks to each table, and a diverse crowd chat happily over stacks of those delicious pancakes.

RUSS & DAUGHTERS CAFE
**Map 2; 127 Orchard Street, Lower East Side; ///super.rider.class;
www.russanddaughterscafe.com**

Sure, the Lower East Side is teeming with Jewish bakeries but it's hard to beat Russ & Daughters, which has fed hungry locals with classic NYC bagels and lox for more than 100 years. The comforting breakfasts and chatty staff will make you feel like part of the family both here and at the store on East Houston Street. Fun fact: this was the country's first business to include "& Daughters" in its name, thanks to progressive owner and father of three, Joel Russ.

SUNDAY IN BROOKLYN
**Map 4; 348 Wythe Avenue, Williamsburg, Brooklyn; ///acted.pitch.over;
www.sundayinbrooklyn.com**

Cool kids flock to this cozy, rustic spot, which has all the vibes of your mom's kitchen. With unfailingly friendly staff and consistently delicious food (think gooey sticky buns and picture-perfect pancakes), Sunday in Brooklyn is the place to return to again and again with your loved ones.
» Don't leave without trying the egg, sausage, and cheese sandwich, a hulking patty topped with crispy, razor-thin potato fries and a creamy aioli dressing.

HOTEL CHANTELLE

Map 2; 92 Ludlow Street, Lower East Side; ///basket.length.hurry;
www.hotelchantelle.com

Stylish professionals and young New Yorkers love to celebrate a
birthday, promotion, or simply welcome the weekend with a boozy
brunch at this fancy rooftop spot. An old-timey band croons jazz
tunes as patrons order rounds of cocktails and eat their way through
portions of chicken and waffles and avocado toast. Thanks to a
retractable roof, brunch carries on rain or shine, so guests can enjoy
the city skyline whatever the weather.

CHEZ MA TANTE

Map 4; 90 Calyer Street, Greenpoint, Brooklyn; ///debate.older.exam;
www.chezmatantebk.com

This classy outpost is famed for its lemony, thick, ultra-rich
pancakes, covered in a layer of char (burnt edges), drenched in
maple syrup, and topped with a square of butter. We're drooling,
too. New Yorkers come from all over the city to dine on these

Try it!
HOMEMADE BRUNCH

Want to wow your friends with a homemade
brunch? The Brooklyn Kitchen in *(www.
thebrooklynkitchen.com)* runs breakfast
pastry classes where you'll make scones,
biscuits, curds, and compotes.

not-your-typical-pancake pancakes, alongside thick-cut fries ("chips") and seasonal fare. Like any savvy local, be sure to make a reservation as it can get incredibly busy.

PEACHES

**Map 4; 393 Lewis Avenue, Bed-Stuy, Brooklyn;
///draw.beside.couch; www.bcrestaurantgroup.com**

Dieters, be warned: the chefs at Peaches cook up Southern comfort food that's meant to fill you up. And with such reasonable prices, you'll find yourself ordering more food than you can handle in one sitting. The food is hearty but the place also has heart; Peaches is committed to serving food sourced from local farmers and producers. It's a spot that feels like home, wherever home may be.

» Don't leave without trying the shrimp and grits, which will take your tastebuds on a journey right down to the Deep South.

TINA'S

**Map 4; 1002 Flushing Avenue, Bushwick, Brooklyn; ///brush.views.worry;
718-497-6890**

You might mistake this as yet another diner that charges hefty New York prices. But, luckily, Tina's bucks the trend. The no-frills diner is all about simple, comforting food that won't cost an arm; where else can you get a full plate of eggs, potatoes, bacon, and toast, plus coffee for $7? It's popular with morning-after-the-night-before partygoers and local workers who want a reliably good breakfast that doesn't break the bank.

Global Grub

This is a city built on immigration, with thousands bringing the flavors of their homeland and heritage to the Big Apple. And the dining scene reflects this rich diversity, with a different cuisine for your every mood.

JONGRO BBQ

Map 3; Floor 2, 22 West 32nd Street, Korea Town; ///parks.oppose.chops; www.jongrobbqny.com

Carnivores, rejoice. Tucked in the heart of the city's small and perpetually busy K-Town is Jongro, king of sumptuous BBQ meats. A meal here is a theatrical affair, with servers grilling and flipping your chosen meats with military-like precision right in front of you. Wash down a decadent feast with a glass of hair-raising Korean *soju*.

IMANI

Map 5; 271 Adelphi Street, Fort Greene, Brooklyn; ///trip.thinks.mugs; www.imaninyc.com

Chef Mohamed Doucoure cooks up a Caribbean storm in the kitchen at Imani. His menu is inspired by his mom's hearty home cooking and, boy, does this show in the generous seasoning and portion sizes. It's all about comfort and being with your loved ones:

In the winter it's worth claiming an outside igloo to stay warm and enjoy the patio culture of Dekalb Avenue. | on weekdays, families chow down on jerk chicken tacos, while on the weekend groups of young people tuck into brunch and glasses of rum punch.

IPPUDO

Map 2; 65 Fourth Avenue, East Village; ///sake.count.veal; www.ippudony.com

Step into Japanese restaurant Ippudo and you'll first be greeted by the bar, which is strategically placed by the entrance to placate those waiting for a table. When there's a free spot you'll be led to one of the communal tables, drink in hand – it's not unheard of to find yourself sitting across from someone you vaguely know, defying all logic of being in a city of millions. Chat to your long-lost friend and watch the chefs working madly in the open kitchen before devouring rich ramen.

WIN SON

Map 4; 159 Graham Avenue, Williamsburg, Brooklyn; ///melt.stable.local; www.winsonbrooklyn.com

This low-key Taiwanese restaurant is the perfect fit in cooler-than-cool Williamsburg. From the outside, Win Son looks like your run-of-the-mill bodega. But inside it's persistently packed and buzzes with diners happily slurping down new-age dishes, like stir-fried tofu and braised beef served in a scallion pancake.

» **Don't leave without** trying the "Sloppy Bao," an overflowing steamed pork bun. Extra points if you don't stain your outfit (seriously, it's sloppy).

Solo, Pair, Crowd

Whether you're grabbing a bite on your own or feasting with your squad, tempting international fare awaits.

FLYING SOLO

Ramen for one

Tucked away in the backstreets of Williamsburg is miniscule Okonomi, where ramen is prepped using every single part of the fish. Get a seat at the kitchen-bar and watch the chefs at work.

IN A PAIR

Catch up over dim sum

Nom Wah Tea Parlor is a Chinatown icon, having opened in 1920. Put your names down and grab a "prescription" at Apotheke *(p61)*, a pharmacy-themed speakeasy next door, before returning for dim sum.

FOR A CROWD

Community plate

Ethiopian meals are built around community and Ras Plant Based brings this ethos to Crown Heights. The sharing plates use organic, local ingredients and will leave you all feeling surprisingly full.

SOMTUM DER

Map 2; 85 Avenue A, Alphabet City; ///olive.lucky.proper;
www.somtumdernewyork.com

Ever heard of Isan cuisine? The regional fare of northeastern Thailand is bursting with flavor, and this trendy East Village space is the place to try it. Regulars in-the-know order the spicy papaya salad, *pad ki mao* (delicate flat rice noodles) and *larb moo* (spicy minced-pork salad).

TOKYO RECORD BAR

Map 1; 127 MacDougal Street, Greenwich Village;
///diary.oddly.fingernails; www.tokyorecordbar.com

Designed like your record-obsessed friend's living room, this tiny subterranean 12-seat restaurant is a dining experience like no other. You're first tasked with choosing two hits, which the DJ mashes up into an upbeat playlist. Your second and ultimate duty: dance in your seat while enjoying the quirky tasting menu of Japanese small plates.

PACIFICANA

Map 6; 813 55th Street, Sunset Park, Brooklyn; ///loses.diner.grows;
www.pacificanabrooklyn.com

Hidden above a dentist's office, in a nondescript shopping plaza, is this authentic dim sum house. Waitstaff roam around the busy hall with an infinite number of tempting plates and pressure guests to order straight away. Sure, it's not the most fancy but the dim sum is second to none.

» Don't leave without ordering some sweet custard buns to round off your banquet. Ask nicely and they'll bag them up for you to take home.

Special Occasion

Birthday? Bachelorette? Bad day? Any and all occasions are marked with a meal in this food-obsessed city. Join locals celebrating their big moments at these memorable spots.

THE DUTCH

Map 1; 131 Sullivan Street, Soho; ///camp.cowboy.slower; www.thedutchnyc.com

The Dutch feels fancy enough to celebrate a birthday or promotion without feeling like you're totally out of your league. Join elegant professionals who populate the bar area for post-work drinks before migrating to a table to tuck into a seafood feast. Even if you don't stay for a full meal, kick-start your celebration with oysters and cocktails at this perennially crowded restaurant. You deserve it.

ABCV

Map 1; 38 East 19th Street, Flatiron District; ///factor.mouse.struck; www.jean-georges.com

Housing a haute-cuisine restaurant inside a home-goods store sounds odd but acclaimed French chef Jean-Georges Vongerichten has made a habit of it, and with great success. After all, this is his third restaurant inside luxury store ABC Carpet & Home. It's also his first vegetarian venture, with a focus on sustainable and organic ingredients from small family farms. Girlfriends flock here for swanky dinners in the pretty, rustic-style space, snapping photos left, right, and centre for their social media. But seriously, the food is delicious; carnivores will be converted to join the plant-based revolution.

BEAUTY & ESSEX

Map 2; 146 Essex Street, Lower East Side; ///jams.silly.chart; www.taogroup.com

Hidden beyond a pawn shop (yep, you read that right) is Beauty & Essex, a sexy speakeasy-restaurant that attracts a steady stream of trendy people looking to splurge their paychecks. Low lighting, dark leather, and a fair amount of velvet upholstery create a swish vibe, which is matched by decadent American small plates. It's the perfect blowout place for high days and holidays.

>> Don't leave without visiting the ladies' bathroom (sorry boys), where there's a tiny champagne bar serving complimentary bubbly all night.

Try it!
MAKE AN ITALIAN FEAST

To make an occasion truly memorable, gather your nearest and dearest and prepare a three-course feast with chefs at Eataly's La Scuola (www.eataly.com). Your party will learn to make pasta, gnocchi, and gelato.

MANHATTA

Map 5; 60th Floor, 28 Liberty Street, Financial District;
///local.grape.shapes; www.manhattarestaurant.com

It's hard to beat a killer view for a special occasion. From its skyscraper
vantage point, Manhatta serves up delicious international fare
alongside stunning, panoramic views of Lower Manhattan. The
dining space is elegant, the food delicious, and the staff are
welcoming, but the star attraction here is New York City itself.

ALTA

Map 1; 64 West 10th Street, Greenwich Village; ///dating.hops.shave;
www.altarestaurant.com

There's a magnetism to Alta, with its rustic interiors and romantic,
orangey glow. Young couples raise champagne flutes as they toast
their anniversaries and small groups of friends chatter over
unhurried feasts of Mediterranean-inspired tapas. If you're looking
to gather all your loved ones for a celebration, go big and order
"The Whole Shebang," which includes everything on the menu.

LAFAYETTE

Map 1; 380 Lafayette Street, Noho; ///trying.swaps.woven;
www.lafayetteny.com

Classic French bistro meets ritzy New York trendsetter at Lafayette.
Waitstaff in suspenders weave around the grand café and dish out
mouthwatering bowls of moules-frites and spaghetti niçoise to
animated groups of patrons. Embrace the leisurely lunch lifestyle

If you want more French vibes, walk a few blocks to Rue B where there's nightly live jazz.

and take advantage of the reasonable $38 midweek prix-fixe menu. Or, if you're planning an alfresco party, pick up some pastries at the adorable attached bakery.

SARAGHINA

Map 4; 350 Lewis Avenue, Bed-Stuy, Brooklyn;
///first.driven.civil; www.saraghina.com

This is the place for a jubilant affair with all the gang. Saraghina does wood-fired pizzas without the exorbitant prices of Zona Rosa or Grimaldi's. Get there before 7pm to make the most of the $8 cocktail happy hour and save a couple of benches for your pals.

» Don't leave without sampling the *polpetta*, a large grass-fed beef meatball, which is more than enough to share with a friend.

UNION SQUARE CAFÉ

Map 1; 101 East 19th Street, Union Square; ///trace.slows.last;
www.unionsquarecafe.com

Business deals have been finalized and Broadway debuts celebrated at Union Square Café since the 1980s. It's basically part of the city's furniture, and every New Yorker feels like they own a piece of the place. Take the restaurant's whopping three-block relocation, which initially shocked locals but proved itself to be just as popular among regulars. The Italian-influenced American cuisine is excellent (think freshly made pasta) and the service impeccable. Get a reservation in for when that promotion is confirmed.

Street Food

Forget about sit-down dinners – nowhere does street food like New York City. From Manhattan's vast food halls to tiny food trucks in Queens, you'll discover a new side of NYC's culinary kaleidoscope.

LOS TACOS NO. 1

Map 3; 229 West 43rd Street, Midtown; ///love.stove.pinch; www.lostacos1.com

You'll struggle to find better tacos anywhere else in the city. Los Tacos No. 1 is an efficient operation, with expert cooks assembling Mexican fare at rapid-fire speed for a constant stream of hungry Times Square workers. Ask the cashier for the off-menu cheese shell, which is exactly what it sounds like: an encasing of fried cheese to replace your tortilla.

AMDO KITCHEN

Map 6; 37–59 74th Street, Jackson Heights, Queens; ///other.edit.yoga; 347-612-8208

This unassuming food truck is run by a former Buddhist monk – cool, right? Based in multicultural Jackson Heights, NYC's epicenter for Tibetan and Nepalese immigrants, Amdo Kitchen is without a doubt one of the best spots to sample *momos* (essentially Nepalese dumplings). The beef *momos* are delicious, especially when smothered in a generous dousing of *sepen*, a red chili sauce. You'll be swinging by Amdo Kitchen again – we'd put money on it.

» Don't leave without traipsing around Jackson Heights for more global culinary delights. Raja Sweets & Fast Food is a good stop-off.

ESSEX MARKET

Map 2; 88 Essex Street, Lower East Side; ///pages.movies.drill;
www.essexmarket.nyc

A collection of open-air pushcarts in the 19th century, Essex Market is today an uber-modern indoor food hall with a glut of specialty shops and stalls. Join city slickers and make a beeline here at lunchtime to sample half-sour pickles from the welcoming Pickle Guys, or Ukrainian pierogies from local favorite Veselka.

Shh!

You know somewhere is a genuine secret when it doesn't have a website. Los Hermanos (718-456-3422) is a tortilleria and taqueria in Bushwick, near the Jefferson L stop. Here you can get three hearty tacos for less than $10, a real feat of a find in trendy and pricey Bushwick. Better still, you can sit right in front of the kitchen and watch the chefs expertly prepare the tortillas, which are supplied to numerous restaurants and bodegas across the city.

TIMEOUT MARKET

Map 5; 55 Water Street, Dumbo, Brooklyn; ///entire.race.bonus;
www.timeoutmarket.com

Come the weekend and the people of Brooklyn gravitate to this market for leisurely afternoons of gorging. The TimeOut Market is packed with spin-offs from some of the city's best-known restaurants, including Mr. Taka, a beloved Lower East Side ramen spot, and Fish Cheeks, an unmissable seafood-centric Soho restaurant. Whatever you go for (and you're spoiled for choice, by the way), enjoy it outside for uninterrupted views over to Manhattan.

MAHMOUD'S CORNER

Map 6; 34th Avenue, Astoria, Queens; ///showed.chefs.jars;
www.mahmouds34thavecorner.weebly.com

Tucked away in Queens, beside a colorful wall of street art, is halal food truck Mahmoud's Corner. A cult following of foodies make pilgrimages to Astoria to sample the truck's Middle Eastern food, most famously the *gyros*, or wraps, which come packed with french fries, eggplant, and a signature sweet sauce.

LE DISTRICT

Map 5; 225 Liberty Street, Brookfield Place, Financial District;
///agents.snow.relate; www.ledistrict.com

Francophiles rejoiced when Le District opened downtown in 2015. Beyond stocking the pain au chocolat and fromage that any respectable Parisian market would have, the food hall also has a gorgeous terrace overlooking the Hudson River. Today, after-work crowds migrate from their Financial District offices for happy-hour drinks, people-watching, and freshly baked bread to take home.

» Don't leave without enjoying a sunset drink at Beaubourg, one of Le District's restaurants, which has a patio with lovely river views.

QUEENS INTERNATIONAL NIGHT MARKET

Map 6; 4701 111th Street, Corona, Queens; ///feel.drama.flute; www.queensnightmarket.com

On Saturday nights, from April through October, Queens celebrates its rich diversity with this market extravaganza. Vendors lovingly prepare Cambodian *amok* (a type of curry), Indian *dosas* and everything in between. Because most items are capped at only $5, visitors mill around for hours, inhaling all the delicious scents and sampling snacks until their stomachs protest. Handily there are globally inspired performances, including all-singing, all-dancing troupes, to entertain throughout the night.

Try it!
MAKE DUMPLINGS

Ukrainian church canteen Streecha *(33 East 7th Street)* makes food for those with a handful of coins in their pocket, with proceeds benefiting the church. Join older local women on Friday mornings to make pierogies.

Sweet Treats

You'd struggle to find an American without a sweet tooth, so it's no surprise that New York City is jam-packed with bakeries, ice-cream parlors, and cheesecake outlets galore.

LEVAIN BAKERY

Map 3; 167 74th Street, Upper West Side; ///apron.clip.shuts; www.levainbakery.com

Spot the line of sugar-addicted New Yorkers and you'll know you've arrived at the right place. Levain is an NYC household name, known for dense, gooey, gigantic cookies that are served warm (with the chocolate still melting). Although the decadent chocolate-chip walnut cookies are the stars of the show, the lesser-known chocolate-chip brioches are also hard to resist.

MORGENSTERN'S FINEST ICE CREAM

Map 2; 2 Rivington Street, Lower East Side; ///loft.cute.cape; www.morgensternsnyc.com

Walking into Morgenstern's feels like stepping back in time. Black-and-white tiled floors and staff in retro-style hats give off all the vibes of a 1950s ice-cream parlor. But one look at the menu,

Nearby Ivan Ramen has a seasonal collab with Morgenstern's – the perfect end to a bowl of noodles.

which has innovative flavors like lavender agave and Vietnamese coffee, and you'll realize this small-batch gem is far from stuck in a timewarp.

OVENLY

Map 4; 31 Greenpoint Avenue, Greenpoint, Brooklyn;
///cube.levels.pint; www.oven.ly

Founded and led by women, this socially responsible Brooklyn bakeshop works to employ underserved populations like refugees, ex-cons, and those living in poverty. It's also dedicated to sustainability and sourcing all-natural, local ingredients whenever possible. Oh, and the baked goods are incredible.

VAN LEEUWEN

Map 2; 48 1/2 East 7th Street, East Village; ///blend.match.bump;
www.vanleeuwenicecream.com

Even on sub-zero winter days you'll see people cocooned in scarves and coats crossing the threshold here for a taste of Van Leeuwen's honeycomb or Earl-Grey-tea ice cream. What began as a single ice-cream truck dedicated to naturally sourced, simple ingredients is now a veritable ice-cream empire with an especially strong vegan following. Line up alongside East Village's hip locals before enjoying your chosen flavor at nearby Tompkins Square Park.

» Don't leave without trying a scoop of the vegan mint chip, one of the many excellent milk-free options.

Liked by the locals

"People always ask what sets our cheesecake apart from others. Our mom raised us in the kitchen and always said three things: 'Don't cut corners; always use the best-quality ingredients; and to make it great, make it with love.'"

HOLLY MALONEY, CO-OWNER AND MANAGER OF EILEEN'S SPECIAL CHEESECAKE

EILEEN'S SPECIAL CHEESECAKE

Map 1; 17 Cleveland Place, Nolita; ///rewarding.fried.bottle;
www.eileenscheesecake.com

New Yorkers are serious about their cheesecake and no shop does it better than Eileen's, which has been serving fluffy, creamy desserts here since the 1970s. The classic flavor is outrageously good, as are specialty flavors, like marble, pumpkin, and s'mores.

PETEE'S PIES

Map 2; 61 Delancey Street, Lower East Side; ///pinks.fingernails.loads;
www.peteespie.com

Walking into Petee's feels like stepping into someone's kitchen: mismatched crockery teeters in stacks, tempting pies are proudly displayed, and friendly staff prepare pastry to feed the masses. This Lower East Side shop (which has a sister store in Brooklyn) does a brisk business, feeding the crowds with delectable sweet pies.

» **Don't leave without** trying the seasonal offering; in fall there's usually a lip-smackingly delicious maple-whiskey walnut pie.

MAGNOLIA BAKERY

Map 1; West 11th Street, 401 Bleecker Street, West Village;
///lights.passes.slimy; www.magnoliabakery.com

If you scoff at the idea of banana pudding, stop by NYC institution Magnolia Bakery, where throngs of happy customers shovel down this creamy treat. Yes it's a chain, and yes *Sex and the City* fans carry out photo shoots outside. But the sweet treats remain top notch.

Comfort Food

We all know this is a city that never sleeps and, let's be honest, it can be exhausting. Warm interiors, friendly faces, and plates of comforting food – these spots are the places to stop for a bit of R & R.

AL DI LA TRATTORIA

Map 5; 248 Fifth Avenue, Park Slope, Brooklyn; ///parts.repay.common; www.aldilatrattoria.com

Outdated wallpaper, a dusty chandelier, and general old-world charm hint that this trattoria has been a neighborhood favorite for years. It's no surprise that Brooklyn families keep coming back to this intimate, no-frills restaurant; its hearty pasta dishes are the perfect medicine on a cold, rainy evening in the city.

JACOB'S PICKLES

Map 3; 509 Amsterdam Avenue, Upper West Side; ///pile.bank.fade; www.jacobs.picklehospitality.com

Sometimes you just need a hearty meal of Southern fare to get you through the day, and for those moments there's Jacob's Pickles. Found next to a leafy neighborhood park, this welcoming spot doles out portions of heart-stopping goodness, like shrimp and bacon grits, mac and cheese, doughy biscuits, and, naturally, the eponymous pickles – all plated up with a side of Southern hospitality. You won't be going for a run after gorging here, trust us.

AUNT JAKE'S

Map 1; 47 West 8th Street, Greenwich Village; ///parks.blows.dine; www.auntjakesnyc.com

When you've got a pasta craving that just won't quit, Aunt Jake's is the answer. This West Village restaurant feels just like home, with its rustic interior and heaped portions of handmade pasta. You can even eat like a kid by indulging in whatever you're feeling that day, thanks to the restaurant's mix-and-match pasta and sauces.

» Don't leave without signing up to a Pasta Lab class so you can learn to cook your own and wow your friends with your new skills.

FERNS

Map 2; 166 First Avenue, East Village; ///awards.pays.senses; www.fernsnyc.com

You can't miss Ferns because, well, its entrance is covered with lush, leafy ferns. Push past the foliage to discover a brick-lined interior, decorated with dangling string lights and, of course, more plants. This East Village spot has an array of personalities: by day, it's a quiet place to grab a casual burger; by night, it transforms into classic date territory thanks to low lighting, live music, and a small-plates menu; on the weekends, it swells with a laid-back crowd of 20- and 30-somethings debriefing on the week's news.

Solo, Pair, Crowd

Is there anything better than getting cozy with comforting food on a miserable day?

FLYING SOLO

Peruvian and people-watching

Grab one of the window seats at trendy Llama Inn, Williamsburg, and watch the world go by as you savor hearty Peruvian food. Follow your meal with a nightcap at the rooftop bar.

IN A PAIR

Banter and burgers

Surely a burger is the best comfort food out there? Head to homey Ruby's Cafe in Soho for a filling Bronte Burger and a proper catch-up. There's also a mean brunch menu.

FOR A CROWD

Sharing plates for four, five, or six

Impress your squad by booking a table at uber-artsy FourFiveSix in Brooklyn. Sink into the thrifty couches, tuck into a banquet of sharing plates, and shoot the breeze.

LA VARA

Map 5; 268 Clinton Street, Cobble Hill, Brooklyn; ///dart.fled.strain;
www.lavarany.com

Whether you're looking to charm a date or you've brought a little
entourage along, sharing is the name of the game at tapas joint
La Vara. This teeny, tiny restaurant serves Spanish small plates with
a Jewish-Moroccan twist. It's the perfect spot to put the world to
rights and rave about the tapas with your favorite people.

RUCOLA

Map 5; 190 Dean Street, Boerum Hill, Brooklyn; ///breed.extra.civil;
www.rucolabrooklyn.com

This is the spot for an overdue catch-up. Inspired by the slow food
movement of Piedmont, Italy, this rustic northern Italian restaurant is a
lovely place to savor good food with good company. Draw up a chair
at one of the long tables and chat over bowls of homemade pasta.

BUVETTE

Map 1; 17 Cleveland Place, West Village; ///rewarding.fried.bottle;
www.ilovebuvette.com

Tucked away on quaint tree-lined Grove Street, Buvette is a bastion
of Parisian charm thanks to the chalkboards and bottles of vino that
line the walls. Grab a late-night meal of simple, hearty French fare
and gorge until closing, several glasses of wine in tow.

» Don't leave without trying the buttery steamed eggs, served with
your choice of ham, salmon, or cheese.

Get creative at
EATALY

Conclude at Eataly – an Italian marketplace – for a pasta-making class, paired with an all-important glass of wine.

*Founded by seven farmers in 1976, **Union Square Greenmarket** has become a staple for New Yorkers seeking fresh farm produce.*

Pay homage to
JOE'S PIZZA

For an authentic NYC experience, scarf down a folded slice of the city's favorite pizza from Joe's Pizza – it's unpretentious and truly iconic.

Settle in at
VESELKA

Still hungry? Stop for a couple of pierogies at this 24/7 Ukranian diner, which is just as busy at noon as 2am, when the post-party crowds stream in.

Amble through
LITTLE TOKYO

Follow your nose as you walk through this 'hood within a 'hood, where sushi joints and bubble tea shops pepper the scene, and the tempting smell of ramen fills the air.

Grab a takeout from
RUSS & DAUGHTERS

Order a bagel and lox sandwich, or a bialy – a doughy bread stuffed with sautéed onions – from this Lower East Side institution.

Soak up the atmosphere in
PAUSE CAFE

Savor a spiced Moroccan coffee or mint tea at this friendly neighborhood café, decorated in Moorish paintings and lanterns.

MADISON SQUARE PARK

GRAMERCY PARK

GREENWICH VILLAGE

Washington Square Park

New York University

UNION SQUARE

EAST VILLAGE

Tampkins Square

PARK AVENUE SOUTH

PARK AVENUE

THIRD AVENUE

SECOND AVENUE

FIRST AVENUE

EAST 14TH STREET

FOURTH AVENUE

EAST 8TH STREET

EAST 9TH ST

EAST 4TH ST

AVENUE A

AVENUE B

FIRST AVE

BROADWAY

EAST HOUSTON STREET

ALLEN ST

0 meters 500
0 yards 500

A day sampling
international flavors

The Lower East Side gets all the glory when it comes to eating out, but the East Village is a pretty strong rival. Its eclectic mix of flavors reflects the wave of immigration that the area saw in the 19th century, when wealthy New Yorkers moved uptown and made way for German, Ukrainian, and Polish immigrants. Today, there's no better way to spend the day, filling up on satisfying flavors as you walk through the Lower East and East Village.

1. Pause Cafe
3 Clinton Street, Lower East Side; www.pausecafenyc.com
///wipe.gallons.ankle

2. Russ & Daughters
179 East Houston Street, Lower East Side; www.russanddaughters.com
///phones.puzzle.gave

3. Veselka
144 Second Avenue, East Village; www.veselka.com
///drag.dates.broker

4. Little Tokyo
Stuyvesant & East 9th streets; East Village
///facing.jabs.code

5. Joe's Pizza
150 East 14th Street, East Village; www.joespizzanyc.com
///bonus.stews.piles

6. Eataly
200 Fifth Avenue, Flatiron District; www.eataly.com
///basis.enhancement.soap

Union Square Greenmarket ///cigar.swung.dirt

DRINK

New Yorkers live much of their lives in the city's bars and cafés. Beers are clinked after work, cocktails are sipped on date night, and lattes are paired with catch-ups on weekends.

Secret Speakeasies

New York's underground speakeasy scene exploded during Prohibition, with revelers cutting loose to jazz and moonshine. Today hidden bars are throwbacks to these times. You've just got to find your way inside.

SAKE BAR DECIBEL

Map 2; 240 East 9th Street, East Village; ///oasis.rests.tools;
www.sakebardecibel.com

A grungy, subterranean sake bar covered in wild, overlapping wall graffiti and bold, discordant art; this is the ultimate cool kids' hangout. Sip your sake – hot or cold, whichever takes your fancy – and look for a free spot on the walls to scribble your own message.

EMPLOYEES ONLY

Map 1; 510 Hudson Street, West Village; ///lamp.marked.meal;
www.employeesonlynyc.com

This is the kind of place to impress a friend or first date. In true secret speakeasy fashion, there's no signage marking the entrance to Employees Only (just look for No. 510) and yet the place buzzes inside, thanks in part to a great 80s soundtrack. Ask for a reading from the in-house psychic, perhaps after sampling the Common Sense cocktail.

67 ORANGE STREET

Map 3; 2082 Frederick Douglass Boulevard, Harlem;
///handle.places.bound; www.67orangestreet.com

This place is a *genuine* secret (the address is a curveball). Based in an old dance hall, which was also one of the city's first Black-owned bars, the speakeasy is decorated with art from the Harlem Renaissance. Draw up a stool and ask the bartender for their best concoction.

APOTHEKE

Map 2; 9 Doyers Street, Chinatown; ///desk.deny.assume;
www.apothekenyc.com

Take the path between Pell Street and Bowery and look for a drab sign that says "Chemist" hanging from a fire escape: you've made it to Apotheke. Inside, mixologists make tried-and-tested "prescriptions" inspired by 19th-century absinthe dens. Get there early, before the masses arrive with their "ailments."

» Don't leave without catching a tantalizing burlesque show. Check out the website for more event details.

Try it!
APOTHEKE ACADEMY

Prefer to mix your own elixir? Then book into Apotheke Academy, where mixologists lead you through the history of the classic cocktail and you'll knock up a few favorites, like an old-fashioned.

RAINES LAW ROOM

Map 1; 48 West 17th Street, Chelsea; ///speak.woof.gown;
www.raineslawroom.com

Ring the doorbell of this sophisticated speakeasy and you'll be ushered into the uber-exclusive-feeling Raines Law Room. Inside, refined couples make eyes at each other in the candlelight and small gatherings of friends sit on low-slung couches, chatting in hushed tones. It's not all class, however. Use the bathroom and look closely at the bathroom's wallpaper – it's surprisingly debaucherous.

POURING RIBBONS

Map 2; 225 Avenue B, Alphabet City; ///menu.rocks.prime;
www.pouringribbons.com

Plopped between a liquor store and an old apartment building, Pouring Ribbons appears like a typically Lower Manhattan walk-up entrance. But push through the doors of this speakeasy and you'll unearth a subtle spot for a drink; the perfect escape from

Shh!

Le Boudoir does what a speakeasy should do: hides in plain sight *(www.boudoirbk.com)*. After all, not many Brooklynites dining in bistro Chez Moi realize there's a bar beneath their feet. Inspired by Marie Antoinette's rooms at Versailles, this cocktail parlor serves the prettiest drinks. Marie Antoinette would approve.

the joie de vivre of Manhattan. It's low-key thanks to the staff
who refrain from packing the bar to capacity, so you'll never need
to yell to chat to your friend (phew). As for the drinks, they're less
subtle and more showy, with great names like Shade, Executive
Realness, and Venus Xtravaganza.

GARFUNKEL'S

Map 2; 67 Clinton Street, 2nd Floor, Lower East Side;
///parade.pulled.lungs; www.garfunkelsnyc.com

By day, Garfunkel's serves afternoon tea, a sophisticated affair with
fancy pastries and finger sandwiches. By night, it transforms into a
sultry cocktail lounge with Prohibition-era vibes. It's classic date
territory, with couples cozying up on the plush velvet couches and
swapping life stories over swanky cocktails.

» **Don't leave without** experiencing the swinging live jazz nights,
held on Tuesdays 8–11pm.

PATENT PENDING

Map 3; 49 West 27th Street, NoMad; ///else.venues.note;
www.patentpendingnyc.com

After an exhausting day at work, Manhattan's office workers traipse
to NoMad's stylish Patent Pending for a much-needed pick-me-up.
Housed in the basement of the Radio Wave Building, where Nikola
Tesla experimented with radio waves in the 1800s, the speakeasy
pays homage to the theme with seasonal cocktails like "Light Me
Up" and "Currents and Coils."

Wine Bars

After a long day or week at work, New Yorkers
find it hard to resist the pull of a fancy wine bar.
Nothing tops drawing up a chair and chatting to an
expert bartender before that first sip of vino.

VIN SUR VINGT

Map 3; 66 West 84th Street, Upper West Side; ///bath.moved.apples;
www.vsvwinebars.com

A play on the French phrase "vingt sur vingt" – or 20 out of 20 – Vin Sur Vingt certainly scores full marks with well-heeled New Yorkers, who like to escape the hectic streets of Manhattan for a taste of France at this cozy bar à vin. Those who find the wine selection overwhelming should consider the Wine Flight, a sampling of three varieties.

D'ANTAN

Map 5; 858 Bergen Street, Crown Heights, Brooklyn;
///shuts.slang.plank; www.dantanbk.com

Serving over 100 varieties by the glass, D'Antan focuses on orange Italian wines and vermouth. The expert waiters are on hand to offer real Italian hospitality, with extensive knowledge of both the wine list and winemakers. It's a great spot for a date, with vintage ceiling

Prefer your drink with live music? There's a jazz show here on Thursdays from 7:30 to 10:30pm.

fans, Polaroids on the walls, and Italian newspapers giving you and your other half the feeling of chilling in an Italian family's kitchen.

JUNE

Map 5; 231 Court Street, Cobble Hill, Brooklyn; ///store.prefer.dwell; www.junebk.com

Everyone seems to know each other at June, with the bartenders joining conversations with hipster locals. The interior of this cute wine bar is welcoming but the back patio is the place to linger, under its twinkling lights. You might as well order a bottle – you'll be here a while.

» Don't leave without sampling one of the refreshing skin-contact wines (aka orange wines), which are basically white wines that haven't had the grape skins removed.

LA COMPAGNIE DES VINS SURNATURELS

Map 1; 249 Centre Street, Nolita; ///miles.fails.cafe; www.compagnienyc.com

This rustically chic bar remains true to the aesthetic of its sister bar, found across the ocean in Paris's 6th arrondissement. Stylish patrons look right at home in the fancy space (it's Nolita, after all) crowding in for happy hour. Want your tasting to be more educational? Check out the Wine Boot Camp, a blind tasting, food pairing, and instruction, meant to take your "Wine Fitness to the next level."

Solo, Pair, Crowd

New York City has a wine bar to suit every occasion, whether you want to sip vino alone or you have the whole squad in tow.

FLYING SOLO

Natural wine for one

Lois, in Alphabet City, is a natural wine bar that serves wine on tap. Chat with the bartender about this concept while enjoying the design-oriented space.

IN A PAIR

Cozy catch-ups

It doesn't get any cozier than Gowanus' Black Mountain Wine House, which looks and feels like a cabin. Catch up with a loved one over a bottle – perfect on a cold night in the city.

FOR A CROWD

Bottles with the gang

Brooklyn Winery in Williamsburg has a relaxed bar attached to the urban winery, with long tables that make for a great get-together. Better still, they do half-priced bottles on Wednesdays.

RED HOOK WINERY

Map 5; 175 Van Dyke Street, Red Hook, Brooklyn; ///yappy.move.export;
www.redhookwinery.com

With an obsession with NYC-born Billy Joel that teeters on
dangerous, and bottles filled on-site with grapes sourced from
growers just upstate, this laid-back and unpretentious tasting room
is just about as New York as it gets. Dog pals are also welcome.

» Don't leave without walking off your wine with a stroll along to
Pier 44, which has stellar views of the Statue of Liberty.

BIBI WINE BAR

Map 2; 211 East 4th Street, Alphabet City; ///scouts.looked.silly;
www.bibiwinebar.com

Don't be fooled by the unassuming exterior of this wine bar. The
welcoming waitstaff really know their wines and, praise be, there's
always a free table. A steady stream of couples, friends, solo drinkers
– you name it – gather for small plates and Bibi's daily happy hour.

RUFFIAN

Map 2; 125 East 7th Street, East Village; ///winner.pads.successes;
www.ruffiannyc.com

Ruffian is a oenophile's dream. With more than 250 selections,
including 30 wines by the glass, budding connoisseurs have plenty
to smack their lips over. And novice drinkers, rest assured: sommeliers
are on hand to wax poetic about different flavors and notes in
each glass before giving you a sample.

Rooftop Bars

A drink tastes better with a great view, right?
The good news is New York has numerous rooftop
bars where the iconic skyline is the perfect backdrop
to a cocktail or bottle of wine.

230 FIFTH

Map 3; 1372 Fifth Avenue, Flatiron District; ///cloak.purely.proper;
www.230-fifth.com

City slickers gravitate toward this seasonally decorated bar, found
20 stories up in the sky, for its I-can't-believe-I-live-here views. The
Empire State Building looks larger than life from the roof's vantage
point and is best admired with a frozen margarita in hand.

» Don't leave without trying the hot chocolate (spiked or virgin, take
your pick) in winter, when the place is occupied with cute igloos.

BOOKMARKS

Map 3; 299 Madison Ave #14, Midtown; ///aura.brass.magma;
www.hospitalityholdings.com

After exploring the New York Public Library it seems appropriate
to walk a couple of blocks to Bookmarks for a literary-themed
aperitif. This rooftop bar is more sedate than many of its big-wig

counterparts but animated conversation still fills the air as intellectuals, bibliophiles, and book groups swap book recommendations over a drink. Chatter to them on the patio and sip creative cocktails like The Pulitzer and The Hemingway; you'll probably leave with an incredible idea for a book of your own.

WESTLIGHT

Map 4; 111 North 12th Street, Williamsburg, Brooklyn;
///monks.parent.blows; www.westlightnyc.com

This is the place to watch the sun set over the waterfront with your NYC family. Found atop Brooklyn's William Vale Hotel, Westlight's chic aesthetic and stellar views make it a popular spot for a special occasion; families celebrate birthdays and groups of friends toast engagements, all the while snapping photographs with the city as a backdrop. Beyond its tempting cocktail list, there's a great menu of small plates to pair with a sky-high drink.

ZONA ROSA

Map 4; 571 Lorimer Street, Williamsburg, Brooklyn;
///future.mull.both; www.zonarosabrooklyn.com

Okay, this little rooftop bar might lack the epic sweeping city views of its rivals but it's still a favorite. Based on the roof of a trailer, Zona Rosa is popular with Williamsburg's down-to-earth locals who cuddle up beneath the heaters in winter and bask in the sunshine in summer, sipping cheap margaritas and people-watching from the roof. The Mexican menu is also top notch.

GALLOW GREEN

Map 3; 530 West 27th Street, Chelsea; ///rent.other.colleague
www.mckittrickhotel.com

McKittrick Hotel isn't your run-of-the-mill New York hotel. For one, it stages *Sleep No More*, an eerily beautiful interactive theater production that's loosely based on *Macbeth*. And then there's its seasonally changing rooftop bar, Gallow Green, inspired by the hotel's enchanting theater production. During the warmer months, this lively bar and restaurant is a green oasis, overflowing with plants and patrons wanting some escapism from the concrete jungle. By winter, the bar transforms into The Lodge, a cozy, rustic space that looks like a cabin in the Scottish Highlands, replete with cozy nooks and flannel galore, plus a menu of wines sourced from June *(p65)*. It's the perfect spot for a wee dram of whiskey or other such nightcap. ,

» **Don't leave without** booking tickets to *Sleep No More*, which takes audience participants through the five-story hotel during the show.

LE BAIN

Map 1; 848 Washington Street, Meatpacking District;
///colleague.palms.rounds; www.standardhotels.com

It's all about being seen at Le Bain. This bi-level rooftop bar, based at the ultra-trendy Standard Hotel, is popular with chic models who hobnob with NYC partygoers. The bar's first level is an enclosed disco-themed space replete with a mini hot tub, which invariably fills as the night goes on. It does have a weird 1970s vibe (not in a good way), so feel free to continue up to the open-air area, which is your typical rooftop hangout. Here, the views of the Hudson and

The Standard Hotel also has a street-level German beer garden, perfect for a more casual drink.

New Jersey are breathtaking, especially at night when the city is lit up. Expect pricey cocktails, DJ sets, and a celebrity sitting at the table opposite.

MR. PURPLE

Map 2; 180 Orchard Street, Lower East Side; ///wants.dive.steep; www.mrpurplenyc.com

Come the weekend and dolled up revelers have one place in mind: Mr. Purple, on the 15th floor of the trendy Hotel Indigo. With two outdoor spaces and long, plush couches to lounge on, Mr. Purple is best enjoyed early to better take advantage of the view and avoid the just-out-of-college crowds – not to mention the line to actually get into the bar in the first place.

CLOUDM ROOFTOP BAR BOWERY

Map 2; 189 Bowery, Lower East Side; ///fans.fence.manual; www.citizenm.com

Groups of friends arriving at 189 Bowery shoot up to the building's 20th floor for CloudM's incredible 360-degree views of the entire city. It's a whimsical and creative space that feels as much like an art gallery as it does a chic bar, thanks to colorful modern art and cool design additions, like New Age Sputnik chandeliers. It's also way more relaxed than other rooftop bars, so you can properly enjoy your drink, a tête-à-tête, and that all important view without feeling intimidated by clubby vibes.

Breweries and Beer Bars

America has been known for its beer production for decades, but the past few years have seen a resurgence of cool breweries and bars that draw an equally cool crowd of beer aficionados.

PROLETARIAT

Map 2; 102 St. Marks Place, East Village; ///moves.sums.monkey;
www.proletariatny.com

In spite of its name, Proletariat is for the discerning craft beer drinker. Expert bartenders will find a "rare, new, and unusual beer" that best suits your palate as you chat to bearded and tattooed regulars, nod your head to great tunes, and generally pre-game for the evening.

BROOKLYN BREWERY

Map 4; 79 North 11th Street, Williamsburg, Brooklyn;
///member.able.translated; www.brooklynbrewery.com

This is a New York City institution, exporting beer to 30 US states and more than 30 countries. Brooklyn Lager might be the favorite but unique formulations are inspired by international flavors, like

Want to learn about the brewing process? There are free tours on weekends; book ahead if you can.

Sorachi Ace, which is inspired by the Japanese brewing process. There's also a hoppy non-alcoholic option if you or a friend are teetotaling.

TØRST

Map 4; 615 Manhattan Avenue, Greenpoint, Brooklyn; ///hero.thick.luck; www.torstnyc.com

Arrive thirsty ("Tørst" is "thirst" in Danish, after all) at this Greenpoint outpost, where you'll find a tempting rotating draft of European and local brews. The airy Scandinavian-inspired taproom is carefully temperature controlled, so your pint will be perfect. If you like what you try, you can also purchase bottle bundles to go.

COVENHOVEN

Map 5; 730 Classon Avenue, Crown Heights, Brooklyn; ///passes.foil.pits; www.covenhovennyc.com

Covenhoven is the type of place where you'll likely run into someone you've seen before. It's a local favorite, where online dates first meet, young parents bounce babies on their knees, and beer lovers unite. The owners live just upstairs – you might spot Bill popping down to sneak a drink or Molly tending to the plants in the garden. The sense of community really is palpable. Don't be afraid to ask to sample before you buy; the bartenders are only too happy to give out tasters.

» **Don't leave without** ordering a grilled cheese sandwich, the perfect accompaniment to a cold beer.

Solo, Pair, Crowd

"Beer is proof that God loves us and wants us to be happy," said Benjamin Franklin. So make merry with your pals, or on your own, at a local brewery.

SOLO
Friends for the night
Always filled with a diverse crowd of Crown Heights locals —and people who wish they'd signed their lease in the neighborhood — Franklin Park is one of the best places to mingle. There's also a vast selection of rotating brews that don't break the bank.

IN A PAIR
Straight outta Deutschland
Loreley Beer Garden in the Lower East Side is modeled on Brauhaus in Cologne, Germany. The outdoor space is heated, which is perfect for a cozy catch-up in winter.

IN A CROWD
Why can't tonight be Oktober?
An endless supply of German beers makes Radegast, in Williamsburg, a great beer hall for a large group. Claim a long table in the beer garden outside as you enjoy a fun fest.

MCSORLEY'S

Map 2; 15 East 7th Street, East Village; ///pretty.windy.eggs;
www.mcsorleysoldalehouse.nyc

This historic ale house and "Irish working man's saloon" has been in business since 1854. It's a small lumber-laden spot with walls covered in news clippings cataloguing NYC history. Don't be surprised if you get caught in the middle of a good old Irish singsong with jolly patrons.

KINGS COUNTY BREWERS COLLECTIVE

Map 4; 381 Troutman Street, Bushwick, Brooklyn; ///dared.major.sides;
www.kcbcbeer.com

Bushwick was once home to Brewer's Row, which comprised 14 breweries, and brewers are bringing the art back to the neighborhood. KCBC is one such brewery, led by brew commanders (their official title, we'll have you know) Tony, Pete, and Zack, who have embarked on many drinking sessions to craft the perfect pint.

» Don't leave without trying the KCBC Plasma Fantasma, which is a rich, berry-infused sour. Refreshing and filling.

CONEY ISLAND BREWERY

Map 6; 1904 Surf Avenue, Coney Island, Brooklyn; ///cases.rotate.trader;
www.coneyislandbeer.com

It's not just about hot dogs and roller-coasters on Coney Island. Oh no. The beachside playground has its very own brewery, with craft beer and table games galore, the perfect spot to cool down with a pint of the signature Mermaid Pilsner after sizzling on the beach.

Dive Bars

Determining the "best" dive bar is a self-defeating task. Should it be the most raucous? The cheapest? The quirkiest? It doesn't matter; dive bars are just about having a good time in well-worn surrounds.

FISH BAR

Map 2; 237 East 5th Street, East Village; ///slam.editor.giant; 917-318-1675

You can still find a $5 pint in Manhattan if you know where to look. Take Fish Bar, an East Village staple that's popular with mature locals who have lived in the neighborhood for decades and like to let their hair down in the familiar surrounds of this local. Visit on the first Saturday of the month for a Beatles-inspired jam session.

BOTANICA

Map 1; 47 East Houston Street, Soho; ///valley.clues.toxic; www.botanicabarnyc.com

When you're looking for a stripped-down spot to kick back in the pomp and polish of downtown's fashion capital, look for the neon sign of Botanica. The peeling paint and exposed weathered brick tell the story of a favorite locale that has been around for a long time. And it's a loud place, as you'd expect from a dive bar. But friendly bartenders will welcome you like an old friend and pour you a reviving pint, and a set of worn leather couches make a lovely spot to rest your weary feet after a long day.

WONDERVILLE

Map 4; 1186 Broadway, Bed-Stuy, Brooklyn;
///gain.mini.spring; www.wonderville.nyc

This is a gamer's paradise. Young friends in slogan T-shirts crowd around pinball machines and other arcade games, often engaging in tournaments with gamers on the next table over. Better yet, the games are free to play (bar a maintenance donation), leaving plenty in the kitty for a round or two of drinks.

» Don't leave without playing Killer Queen, a ten-player strategy game that will leave you with a whole new group of friends.

ROCKY MCBRIDE'S

Map 6; 27–01 23rd Avenue, Astoria, Queens; ///waddled.cost.sugar;
www.rockymcbrides.com

New Yorkers generally love sport but Queens residents in particular are fanatics. They flock in their droves to Rocky McBride's on game day, in need of affordable drinks and a crowd of sympathetic fans. Join them at this Astoria bar when the Yankees or Giants are playing, or for a US soccer match, and swing on the emotional pendulum with the friends you'll make. This spot is a straight-up watering hole and sports fan heaven with over 30 TVs, cheap beer, and drinking games galore.

MARIE'S CRISIS

Map 1; 59 Grove Street, Greenwich Village; ///clues.served.trio;
www.mariescrisis.us

Forget about Broadway. *This* is the place for a night to remember. Under a canopy of Christmas lights stands a piano where, each night, a new musician tickles the ivories as a crowd of carefree drinkers belt out classic show tunes. It's popular with the LGBTQ+ community and anyone looking to make a friend in the city.

RUDY'S BAR & GRILL

Map 3; 627 Ninth Avenue, Hell's Kitchen; ///cage.chips.years;
www.rudysbarnyc.com

One of the first bars to get a liquor license when Prohibition ended, Rudy's was favored by the likes of Al Capone and Frank Sinatra. And people still turn up here like they're finally allowed to drink in public again. The lights are dim, the vibe is boisterous, and the drinks are cheap. Not to mention that each drink comes with a free hot dog – perfect for a late-night stop in.

SUNNY'S BAR

Map 5; 253 Conover Street, Red Hook, Brooklyn; ///brand.looks.cove;
www.sunnysredhook.com

Sunny's is one of a kind and a true New York treasure. Yes, Brooklyn is famously gentrifying but this old-school saloon has held on to its charm, with inimitable live bluegrass and honky-tonk performances every day of the week. A new generation of cool kids pile in to this

While you're in Red Hook, make for Mexican-themed San Pedro Inn, which is divey by design.

Red Hook dive bar to sit close up to the band and forget their troubles. There's also a quaint little backyard for sultry summer nights.

SKINNY DENNIS

Map 4; 152 Metropolitan Avenue, Williamsburg, Brooklyn;
///text.body.pinch; www.skinnydennisbar.com

To find an authentic slice of country look no further than this Billyburg dive bar. A casual honky-tonk joint right off trendy Berry Street, the bar is named for country music bassist "Skinny" Dennis Sanchez, who stood at 6'11" (2.1 m) and weighed 135 lbs (61 kg). The spirit of Skinny lives on thanks to regular performances and a vintage jukebox.

JULIUS'

Map 1; 159 West 10th Street, Greenwich Village; ///spent.cycles.steps;
www.juliusbarny.com

First opened as a grocery store in 1840, Julius' is thought to be the oldest gay bar in New York City. Like nearby Stonewall Inn, the bar is listed on the National Register of Historic Places thanks to its 1966 "sip-in," which was inspired by a Civil Rights sit-in in the South and ultimately led to LGBTQ+ bars being legalized. Today a diverse clientele sit up at the bar to shoot the breeze and chow down on Julius' famous, juicy burgers. Saturday night is dance night, just so you know.

» Don't leave without stopping by the Stonewall National Monument, one block south on Seventh Avenue.

Coffee Shops

New Yorkers have an intimate – borderline obsessive – relationship with caffeine. Thankfully, whether they're ordering a grab 'n' go cup or enjoying a leisurely weekend latte, there's a coffee shop for every occasion.

BLACK CAT LES

Map 2; 172 Rivington Street, Lower East Side; ///ranks.fuzzy.moss; www.blackcatles.com

When the rain is lashing down, Black Cat LES is the perfect place to curl up in an oversized chair and sip a comforting mug of coffee. You'll probably spot a Rachel or Joey type, stationed on the oversized furniture for hours. By night, the living-room-esque setup transforms into an intimate event space, where neighbors gather for comedy and movie event nights. Could a coffee shop be any more cozy?

DEVOCIÓN

Map 4; 69 Grand Street, Williamsburg, Brooklyn; ///owners.busy.steep; www.devocion.com

The rich aroma of Colombian beans is the first thing to greet you when entering Devoción. Follow the scent past the industrial roasting machinery to the main coffee shop, which is a lovely airy space (downright huge by New York standards) with sun dripping down from an enormous skylight and a soaring vertical garden covering the back wall. This Williamsburg store is an eternally crowded hipster paradise, with home workers tapping furiously at laptops day through to night.

UGC EATS
Map 3; 1674 Park Avenue, Harlem; ///lock.deny.method; www.ugceats.com

Colorful and quirky UGC Eats feels entirely lived in, like a kooky extension of your home. The space is packed with a collection of incongruous bric-a-brac: model ships stand on shelves, illuminated street-crossing signs perch behind the counter, potted plants are peppered across surfaces, and garage sale-like furniture populates the café. The vibe is similarly relaxed, with locals making small talk, reading, and knitting as they sip on mochaccinos.

>> Don't leave without sampling the olive oil cake, a delightful, spongy, not-too-sweet slice of goodness, perfect to pair with a frothy latte.

ABRAÇO
Map 2; 81 East 7th Street, East Village; ///enable.lanes.blaze; www.abraconyc.com

With a strictly enforced no-laptop, no-wifi policy, this homey, cash-only espresso bar forces you to get off your devices and back to basics. Groups of trendy East Villagers gather in the simply decorated shop, and they return again and again for the top-shelf coffee, sourced from all over the world. Oh, and the pastries. Delicious, yummy pastries.

DTUT

Map 3; 1744 Second Avenue, Upper East Side; ///fight.rushed.pills;
www.dtutcafe.com

Students and remote workers create a collective hum of keyboard tapping and page turning during the day in effortlessly cool DTUT. The shop is all about community thanks to the ethos of owner Corey, who commissioned all the store's gorgeous mugs from a local artist.
» Don't leave without raiding DTUT's collection of board games, which includes Cards Against Humanity.

COFFEE PROJECT NY

Map 2; 239 East 5th Street, East Village; ///matter.looked.ahead;
www.coffeeprojectny.com

This little shop is created by, and for, coffee geeks. It subscribes to the no-laptop policy, meaning you can chat with friends in this simple, brick-lined space without competing with digital nomads. Try the deconstructed latte: a shot of espresso, shot of whole milk, and a perfectly "ratio-ed" latte, lined up in a picture-worthy trio.

LITTLE ZELDA

Map 5; 728 Franklin Avenue, Crown Heights, Brooklyn;
///backs.moods.violin; 347-378-2915

The best things come in small packages. Take Little Zelda, which seems to have been plucked from a backstreet of Paris with it's rickety furniture, collection of dog-eared books, and plinky plonky soundtrack. Order a coffee and enjoy outside on the plant-covered sidewalk.

Liked by the locals

"DTUT is by far the coziest coffee shop on the UES. I go for the plush couches and coffee and stay for the alcohol and s'mores. It's perfect for a rainy Saturday when you want to feel like you're in a New York-based sitcom."

RENNA GOTTLIEB, TEACHER AND COFFEE ADDICT

**Raise a glass at
MAYAMEZCAL**

Sample Mexican fare and
mezcal-based cocktails at this
low-lit spot, featuring over
60 mezcal and tequilas.

The **Museum of the
American Gangster**
*is housed in a former
speakeasy and is packed
with exhibits from
the Prohibition era.*

Tompkins
Square

EAST

EAST 7TH STREET

6TH STREET

EAST
VILLAGE

**Get cozy at
LOVERS OF TODAY**

Grab a post-dinner drink at this
miniscule, basement cocktail
lounge filled with 20-somethings
enjoying quality cocktails.

BOWERY

SECOND AVENUE

FIRST AVENUE

AVENUE A

AVENUE B

EAST

EAST
4TH STREE

EAST HOUSTON STREET

EAST

2ND STREET

STANTON STREET

STREET

ELDRIDGE STREET

STREET

ALLEN

RIVINGTON STREET

NORFOLK STREET

The Back Room *is
a Prohibition-era
speakeasy still open
today. It serves its drinks
in pretty teacups.*

**Nightcap at
ATTABOY**

A gray, unmarked door may be
all you see from the outside, but
dare to knock, and you'll be
rewarded with some of NYC's
best bespoke cocktails.

DELANCEY STREET

LOWER
EAST SIDE

③
Enjoy some music at
RUE B
Ready to face the music?
Hit up Rue B, a snug jazz
bar with live music and
specialty cocktails.

EAST
9TH
STREET

**ALPHABET
CITY**

EAST
7TH
STREET

AVENUE C

An evening of cocktails in
the East Village

Prohibition may be a thing of the past but the
reign of the speakeasy is far from over in NYC.
Make a beeline for the East Village and you'll
find an array of secret, and not-so-secret, bars –
some old, some new, some still a little seedy.
You'll discover a good dollop of 1920s history
here too; this was gangster territory, after all.
Come the evening, the streets here buzz with
young professionals on the hunt for post-work
drinks, but as the night goes on, the party starts
to move underground – so keep an eye out for
those secret staircases.

1. Mayamezcal
304 East 6th Street, East
Village; www.mayamezcal.
com ///eating.spike.chef

3. Rue B
188 Avenue B, East Village;
www.rueb-nyc.com
///whites.chained.transit

2. Lovers of Today
132 1/2 East 7th Street, East
Village; www.loversoftoday
nyc.com ///scarf.joins.handle

4. Attaboy
134 Eldridge Street, Lower
East Side; www.attaboy.us
///hurry.agent.marble

📍 **Museum of the American Gangster** ///bottom.atomic.sounds

📍 **The Back Room** ///charmingly.factor.pigs

0 meters   250
0 yards   250

SHOP

Forget fast fashion and department stores: New Yorkers love snapping up one-off pieces for their wardrobe and apartment, from cool vintage apparel to quirky home goods.

Vintage Gems

Ever the trendsetters, New Yorkers love to reuse past fashions and furniture to make their look unique. Manhattan has a glut of vintage shops, but Brooklyn is the place for a real treasure hunt.

MR. THROWBACK
Map 2; 437 East 9th Street, East Village; ///silly.noting.means;
www.mrthrowback.com

This shop might be truly miniscule but it's bursting with vintage sports apparel handpicked by 90s-obsessed Michael Spitz aka Mr. Throwback. The store's philosophy is to curate sportswear and paraphernalia that'll remind shoppers of their childhoods (think baseball caps, basketball jerseys, windbreakers, WWF figurines). Step inside and you'll feel like you're back in your childhood bedroom.

BEACON'S CLOSET
Map 5; 92 Fifth Avenue, Park Slope, Brooklyn; ///dock.serves.driven;
www.beaconscloset.com

You can't talk about NYC thrifting and not mention Beacon's Closet, a female-founded vintage bazaar business that has four locations across the city. The Park Slope shop is undoubtedly the coolest, with

Here in summer? Brooklyn Flea features vintage clothes, antiques, and street food on weekends. hip Brooklyn moms and fashion-forward students digging through the substantial array of clothes, shoes, and accessories, before triumphantly exiting with their finds.

CURE THRIFT SHOP

Map 2; 111 East 12th Street, East Village; ///cubes.towers.zips; www.curethriftshop.com

Quirky Cure Thrift Shop is a kaleidoscope of fashion (with vintage furniture thrown in for good measure). Gaggles of excited girlfriends spend hours here, picking through ostentatious coats and modeling antique jewelry for each other. Beyond the wonderful style selections, this shop also has an important mission as a nonprofit, with proceeds benefiting diabetes research and advocacy.

» Don't leave without walking one avenue over to East Village Thrift Shop, yet another small storefront packed with recycled clothes.

10 FT SINGLE BY STELLA DALLAS

Map 4; 285 North 6th Street, Williamsburg, Brooklyn; ///money.lies.hang; 718-486-9487

Whichever area of the city you're in, you'll see 30-somethings donning pre-loved Levi's, army fatigues, and athletic jackets. Chances are these fashion gems were picked up at 10 ft Single by Stella Dallas. This treasure trove also stocks all manner of accessories. Lost that bow tie your grandma gave you? Or hankering after a "new" pair of sunglasses for the summer? This place has got you covered.

MONK VINTAGE

Map 4; 37 Greenpoint Avenue, Greenpoint, Brooklyn; ///bill.green.wiser; 718-384-6665

If you have an upcoming costume party, need an oddball accessory, or just want to add another garish sweater to your collection, head to Monk Vintage. Popular with New York's kooky fashionistas, this thrift shop is packed to capacity with used men's and women's clothing. Yes, it will take time to sift through the eclectic collection and wacky t-shirts, but with stamina and a discerning eye, you'll undoubtedly find hidden wonders, like a kitsch shirt from the 70s.

THE BIG REUSE

Map 5; 12th Street, Gowanus, Brooklyn; ///snacks.soaks.slowly; www.bigreuse.org

Cool couples frequent this enormous warehouse, running their fingers along century-old chairs, mottled mirrors, and vintage whiskey glasses as they imagine transforming their tiny rental. All the store's goods are donated and they're rotated constantly,

Try it!
SEW A QUILT

Americans love their quilts – the more patterned the better. Save your old shirts, bedding, and dishcloths, and book onto a quilt-making class at Gotham Quilts (www.gothamquilts.com).

which means it's sensible to buy then and there – especially as most items sell for a pittance and so are quickly snapped up. There's no better souvenir of your time in the Big Apple than a funky vase or platter that previously graced a New Yorker's apartment.

AWOKE VINTAGE

Map 4; 132 North 5th Street, Williamsburg, Brooklyn;
///shrimp.tell.beside; www.awokevintage.com

Neatly organized into color brackets, the vintage clothing in this cute shop gives off all the airs and graces of high-end design. A regular and devoted crowd of Williamsburg trendsetters comb the rails in this bright and airy store, hunting for the perfect pair of recycled jeans or a one-off colorful beanie. It's no wonder the store has partnered with various designers and production companies.

HOUSING WORKS

Map 1; 130 Crosby Street, Soho; ///exams.pads.reader;
www.housingworks.org

This thrift shop and its neighboring bookstore form part of a beloved nonprofit working to fight AIDS and homelessness in the city. There's a lovely community feel here, thanks largely to the volunteer staff who are, surely, among the friendliest in the city and are only too happy to help you source some new items for your closet.

» Don't leave without visiting the sister bookstore and its café (which you'll want to photograph, it's such a beautiful space) to buy a book and beverage before catching a Moth StorySLAM storytelling event.

Book Nooks

*Bookstores are the heart of the city's neighborhoods.
They're spaces for honoring great literature, engaging
in bookish discussions, pushing boundaries, and
offering refuge for absolutely everyone.*

BOOK CULTURE

Map 3; 2915 Broadway, Morningside Heights; ///slick.light.dined; www.bookculture.com

Cerebral college students comb the shelves of Book Culture,
handily located just across the street from Columbia University.
Follow the behavior of future leaders and novelists and enjoy a
browse yourself. If you're feeling adventurous, pick one of the "Blind
Date Books," a wrapped book with notes from the staff explaining
who this "mystery" selection is best for. It'll beat any human date.

MCNALLY JACKSON

Map 1; 52 Prince Street, Nolita; ///fairly.hours.cats; www.mcnallyjackson.com

Expertly curated shelves, novels hanging from the ceiling, and
knowledgeable staff all make McNally Jackson a haven for book
lovers. The first-floor fiction is uniquely organized by author

nationality and peppered with intriguing "staff favorites," which results in visitors striking up lengthy, meandering conversations with the heartfelt booksellers. The store also has a lovely café where shoppers take stock of their spoils, whether that's a small-press novel or a sizzling summer read.

» **Don't leave without** buying some gorgeous stationery or a notebook to pen your own bestseller.

THE LIT. BAR

Map 6; 131 Alexander Avenue, Mott Haven, The Bronx;
///gent.jukebox.trial; www.thelitbar.com

This Black, female-owned business is a special place. It's filled an important void in the borough, what with being the only bookstore in the Bronx and, as a result, a refuge for bookworms. After buying a book (or three), grab a drink at the store's lovely wine bar — owner Noëlle Santos rightly believes every book purchase deserves a toast — where the counter is decorated with hundreds of books.

BOOKS ARE MAGIC

Map 5; 225 Smith Street, Cobble Hill, Brooklyn; ///fever.unwanted.guises;
www.booksaremagic.net

Literary celeb Emma Straub (of *The Vacationers* and *Modern Lovers*) opened this small shop after her local bookstore closed. The indie shop has become a Cobble Hill staple, with toddlers pulling their parents toward the hidey hole, intellectuals booking spots at author talks, and millennials snapping pictures of the striking mural outside.

UNNAMEABLE BOOKS

Map 5; 600 Vanderbilt Avenue, Prospect Heights, Brooklyn; ///cure.entire.rounds; 718-789-1534

If you prefer your bookshelf to be lined with both new and pre-loved paperbacks, Unnameable Books is the place for you. The Brooklyn Heights indie store is especially popular with local progressives who rifle avidly through the store's eclectic secondhand collection and attend meetings and lectures held in the store.

COMMUNITY BOOKSTORE

Map 5; 143 Seventh Avenue, Park Slope, Brooklyn; ///settle.weedy.layers; www.communitybookstore.net

Shelves teeter with titles for both adults and children at this beloved Park Slope haunt. Bookworms, both young and old, armed with tote bags, head here for the wonderful program of events, including a

Bookstores aren't only above ground, you know. In the basement of New York Public Library outpost Webster Library *(www.nypl.org)*, in the Upper East Side, you'll find the Book Cellar, an unassuming spot for discounted books, which is run by volunteers. The selection varies, what with all the books being donated, but there's nothing more thrilling than salvaging a stack of bargain-basement-priced novels. The best part? All proceeds go back to the library system.

book club, writing workshops, and conversations with authors like Patti Smith and Judd Apatow. A newer outpost, Terrace Books, opened in 2013 on the other side of Prospect Park.

» Don't leave without keeping an eye open for Tiny the Usurper, the store cat, who is especially partial to salmon (hint hint).

KINOKUNIYA
Map 3; 1073 Sixth Avenue, Midtown; ///relax.city.crib; www.kinokuniya.com

This is the place to geek out on everything Japanese. While the main floor consists of books – particularly beautiful coffee-table tomes – the basement is a crafter's dream come true as it features gorgeous Japanese papers and stationery. Head to the top floor and you'll find a manga and anime paradise, along with an attached café.

WESTSIDER RARE AND USED BOOKS
Map 3; 2246 Broadway, Upper West Side; ///branch.spared.erase; www.westsiderbooks.com

We think this store is particularly special. Why? Crossing the threshold is like entering the apartment of some eccentric book-buying addict. Floor-to-ceiling bookshelves greet you, the upper echelons accessible only by wooden ladder; even more books are stacked precariously along the staircase leading up to the store's tiny mezzanine. This is the place for hidden, out-of-print treasures, unexpected oldies, and that unmistakable, musty scent of volumes that have lived through many years. You won't be able to leave empty-handed.

Record Stores

Ella Fitzgerald, the Rat Pack, the Ramones, Run DMC, Lady Gaga. Surely NYC boasts the most incredible and diverse music history? Dig the crates of these record stores and unearth a musical gem for yourself.

ACADEMY RECORDS

Map 4; 85 Oak Street, Greenpoint, Brooklyn; ///head.always.slows; www.academy-lps.com

This crate diggers' mecca in Greenpoint is so vast and varied that you could spend days trawling through its records. Here you'll find enviable collections of world music, disco classics, and moshpit-worthy metal, plus everything in between. It's especially buzzy on weekends when old rockers and young ravers arrive in their droves to spend hours here, all looking to part with their paycheck.

ROUGH TRADE

Map 3; 30 Rockefeller Plaza, 6th Avenue, Midtown; ///over.movie.chief; www.roughtradenyc.com

No stranger to hosting a great party, Rough Trade is the king of record stores. The Rough Trade label was founded in London in the 1970s and, ever since, the name has struck a chord with music lovers. Today, a grungy crowd of hardcore music lovers and newbie turntable owners gravitate to the store, which is appropriately just a stone's throw from the iconic Radio City Music Hall. It's worth checking the website for any big upcoming events, or simply chance your luck and hang around after shopping – surprise, intimate gigs sometimes pop up here.

A1 RECORD SHOP
Map 2; 439 East 6th Street, East Village; ///head.swift.vest; 212-473-2870

Standing strong for a couple of decades, A1 Records will show you why its loyal following of crate diggers come back again and again. It's a favorite among DJs – both experienced old-timers and gutsy newcomers – who rely on the store's second-hand collection of jazz, funk, house, and hip-hop, not forgetting the friendly staff who are always happy to chat all things music.

» Don't leave without taking a look at the store's fading Polaroids. You'll spot the likes of DJ Premier and New York legend DJ Tony Touch.

Try it!
BECOME A DJ

Always dreamed of becoming a DJ? Learn to scratch and mix with Rock and Soul, in Midtown. It runs in-store and virtual classes, which you can do solo or with your friends (*www.rockandsoul.com*).

CAPTURED TRACKS

Map 4; 195 Calyer Street, Greenpoint, Brooklyn; ///rugs.hardly.follow;
www.omnianmusicgroup.com

Don't be fooled by the small stature of this shop, hidden in a residential block; like the TARDIS, there's way more on the inside. Captured Tracks is a haven for indie rock lovers, while the cassette tapes (they're revived and oh-so-trendy here) attract those obsessed with all things 90s.

STRANDED RECORDS

Map 2; 218 East 5th Street, East Village; ///boss.nods.broad;
www.strandedrecords.com

The good people behind the Superior Viaduct record label bring you this slick, pastel-pink store. Music choices are largely outside of the mainstream, tempting a wonderfully diverse crowd of young music fans on the lookout for eclectic new tunes.

BROOKLYN RECORD EXCHANGE

Map 4; 599 Johnson Avenue #1, Bushwick, Brooklyn;
///define.unique.pies; www.brooklynrecordexchange.com

It might look makeshift, with plywood walls and exposed lightbulbs, but this store is anything but. Aside from the fact that it houses every genre under the sun, and many records for just $10, there's a community feel about the place. The staff have an encyclopedic music knowledge, and you can sell your own records on to hipster Brooklynites.

» Don't leave without perusing the collection of sci-fi paperbacks – the perfect accompaniment to a newly purchased soundtrack.

Liked by the locals

"The New York music scene has an energy unlike anywhere else because it has historically been the originator of so many new forms of music. You can feel the history in the scene today and in the underground artists and communities that work to keep the legacy alive."

KAT ARNETT, LEGAL ASSISTANT AND
RECORD STORE SHOPPER

Home Touches

*New Yorkers love personalizing their homes –
however cramped the space is – with quirky art,
too-pretty-to-burn candles, and fun kitchenware.
And you can buy a bit of NYC to take home, too.*

THE GEORGE GLAZER GALLERY

**Map 3; 308 East 94th Street, Upper East Side; ///seat.soil.active;
www.georgeglazer.com**

Corporate attorney George Glazer left the law to pursue his real
passion: collecting antique globes, prints, and maps. And so this
wonderland of relics was born. A creaking antiquarian shop, the
George Glazer Gallery is where eccentrics come to pour over all
sorts of rarities. And whether you're a serious or newbie collector,
be comforted that the antique store is adept at modern shipping.

CRYSTALS GARDEN

**Map 2; 247 East 10th Street, East Village; ///chin.await.lend;
www.crystalsgardennyc.com**

This wonderfully psychedelic shop, with its dizzying array of plants
and crystals, prides itself on dishing out good vibes for the home.
Greenery covers the space from floor to ceiling, incense hangs in

the air, and a rhythmic soundtrack keeps the store's kooky shoppers in a chilled, meditative state. And if you look at those shoppers closely, you'll see them wearing the spiritually charged jewelry while they browse the range of healing crystals. Crystals Garden is truly sacred ground for those with a penchant for spirituality and metaphysics.

» Don't leave without treating yourself to a teeny-tiny terrarium-encased cacti, the perfect way to brighten up any space.

COMING SOON
Map 2; 53 Canal Street, Lower East Side; ///stops.jumped.oldest; www.comingsoonnewyork.com

When New Yorkers need a birthday gift for a friend, or want to add that je ne sais quoi to their apartment, this trendy home-goods store is the place they go to. Everything that Coming Soon stocks – gorgeous multicolored candles, Jackson Pollock-esque plant holders, funky hourglass sets – is artsy, cool, and slightly over your budget. The dopamine-inducing colors and creative designs are just too hard to resist.

Shh!

To infuse your home with a touch of literal NYC magic, check out Enchantments *(www. enchantmentsincnyc.com)*.

It's the city's oldest occult store, dealing in incense and custom-carved candles that are sure to bring good fortune to your home.

GOODS FOR THE STUDY

Map 1; 50 West 8th Street, Greenwich Village; ///punks.plot.rushed; www.goodsforthestudy.com

Creatives and home workers love this office supply store, fantasizing about their dream desk space as they carefully place notebooks, planners, and pens galore into their overflowing basket. The sleek-yet-homey shop has an entire wall covered in color-coordinated pen varieties: ballpoint, rollerback, felt tip – the list goes on.

COLLYER'S MANSION

Map 5; 179 Atlantic Avenue, Cobble Hill, Brooklyn; ///slime.family.speaks; www.shopthemansion.com

It's all about dopamine for the home at Collyer's Mansion, where colorful and patterned homewares are stacked every which way you turn. Attracting chic Brooklynites hunting for that next striking piece for their apartment, here you'll find woven baskets, ceramic plant holders, and cotton dish cloths – all in a glorious splash of color.

SIMPLE GOODS

Map 4; 346 Bedford Avenue, Williamsburg, Brooklyn; ///meals.dined.dating; www.simplegoodsbrooklyn.com

Tiny Williamsburg concept store Simple Goods showcases a combination of locally made goods and pieces by international artisans. Although the stock and space might be small, the striking rugs, hand-poured candles, and lovely scent collection make this a charming and calming spot to visit. After shopping,

Head two blocks over to BEAM for modern homeware, including hand-blown glassware and cool lighting.

stop on the adjoining café's patio and peruse the North African-European-New York menu, which, in itself, is very NYC. The brunch is especially good.

THE OLD PRINT SHOP

Map 3; 150 Lexington Avenue, Murray Hill; ///thank.shine.topic;
www.oldprintshop.com

You could spend hours wandering around this treasure-packed shop, which was founded way back when in 1898. Specializing in overlooked American prints and antiquarian maps, it's the place to find a piece of art to take home – whether you're after a brooding 20th-century print of iconic Midtown or a hazy, romantic take on sunrise in Brooklyn by a contemporary artist.

FISHS EDDY

Map 1; 889 Broadway, Flatiron District; ///petal.broker.easy
www.fishseddy.com

You'd struggle to find a New Yorker who doesn't have a piece of whimsical crockery from Fishs Eddy, which has been flogging quirky kitchenware since the 80s. Forget "I Love NY" mugs; this is the place to pick out quality New York-themed stuff to remember your stay in the Big Apple and stock up on gifts for your loved ones, like a Brooklyn dish towel for your mom or a skyline shot glass for your best friend.

» Don't leave without window-shopping at luxury home-goods store ABC Carpet & Home just across the street.

US Design

New York is a fashion mecca, with locals looking beyond the big-name, designer shops in favor of the true gems: independent, unexpected stores, where each piece of apparel feels like a well-kept secret.

ASSEMBLY NEW YORK

Map 2; 170 Ludlow Street, Lower East Side;
///vibe.cheeks.famous; www.assmblynewyork.com

This is where well-heeled locals come for capsule pieces to modernize their closets. White wooden flooring, clothing rails arranged at angles, accessories displayed on plinths; Assembly New York is like a gallery. Hardly surpising as owner Greg Armas was a gallerist. And the pieces here are like artworks – expertly designed and beautifully made.

L'APPARTEMENT SÉZANE

Map 1; 254 Elizabeth Street, Nolita; ///hook.prime.boots;
www.sezane.com

Chic New Yorkers descend on this Nolita boutique, which carries upscale, French-cool-girl-inspired clothes and accessories. The store's design is inspired by its founders' stylish French apartment and aims to be a space where women feel at home to peruse elegant,

Want a scent for your new look? At Olfactory NYC, a block away, you can make your own unique perfume.

timeless apparel. Beyond the irresistible offerings, the store also partners with nearby French bakery Maman, so you can refuel with a coffee after shopping.

SINCERELY, TOMMY

Map 4; 343 Tompkins Avenue, Bed-Stuy, Brooklyn; ///plug.fade.vague; www.sincerelytommy.com

It's hard to find a fashionista who doesn't adore Sincerely, Tommy. The brainchild of Bed-Stuy native Kai Avent-deLeon, the store is all about celebrating the neighborhood that informed Kai's own sense of style. It stocks a mix of Brooklyn-based and far-flung designers who excel at clean lines and neutral tones. And there's a just a lovely, inclusive feeling about the place. Stop by for a browse and a latte in the store's little coffee bar.

LA DI DA DEE

Map 4; 225 Grand Street, Williamsburg, Brooklyn; ///castle.forest.plans; www.ladidadee.com

This adorable Williamsburg shop is "inspired by the Brooklyn girl": feminine, edgy, and bright. And its wonderfully curated selection of clothes, accessories, and jewelry very much hits that mark, with an array of flirty, cool finds that your trendy best friend would approve of. More good news: the unique designs are also affordable.

» Don't leave without taking at look at the home goods, which are all eco-conscious and all-round beautiful.

KITH

Map 1; 337 Lafayette Street, Soho; ///unrealistic.firm.earth;
www.kith.com

Shoe aficionados will know – or are about to become obsessed with –
this New York-based streetwear brand, known for its trendy sneakers.
Its own selection aside, this brand regularly collaborates with big
fashion names (Levi's, Nike, etc.). Ultimately, this is a cool kids' paradise.
» **Don't leave without** popping by Kith Treats, the store's cereal-
based ice-cream counter. "The 80" is particularly tasty.

KREWE

Map 1; 85 1/2 Spring Street, Soho; ///poem.badge.timing;
www.krewe.com

New Orleans-based luxury brand Krewe has a unique collection
of eyewear, available at its one New York brick-and-mortar store.
Splurge on well-crafted, delicate sunglasses and be rest assured

Shh!

Friends, we'll let you in on a little
secret. Ring the buzzer at 158
Rivington Street to gain access
to Alife Rivington Club *(www.
alifenewyork.com)*. It's like
entering the shoe closet of
Kingsman. You'll be greeted by
row upon row of individually
lit sneakers, each in their own
wood-paneled cubbyhole. Take
a pew on the leather couch and
take your time trying pairs on.
Only those in-the-know come
here, so you won't feel rushed.

that few others will be sporting these cool, Southern-style frames. A bonus fact for pop-culture buffs: the brand has been spotted on stylish celebrities like Beyoncé and Adam Driver.

TAGS

Map 4; 76 North 4th Street, Williamsburg, Brooklyn;
///comic.hungry.goat; www.tags.com

Travelers: New York has a store for you, filled with simple, comfortable, trendy clothes ideal for hopping on a plane or embarking on a road trip. Founded by a former Foreign Service kid, who went on to have kids of her own and is constantly taking them off on adventures, TAGS aims to make packing easy and light, with easy-to-wear basics. But the "simple" aesthetic doesn't mean boring; this Williamsburg shop has an enticing selection of fashionable finds, like utilitarian weekend duffels, knit sweaters, and sleekly cut blazers.

BELIEF

Map 6; 2401 29th Street, Astoria, Queens; ///shells.ears.sing
www.shop.beliefnyc.com

Skateboarders, you don't have to compromise on your look. This indie store does clothing that's made to withstand the wear and tear of skating the streets (all apparel is made from premium materials), while also keeping you looking fresh. Fancy some new slogan tees? Or a sweatshirt for fall? Belief has got you covered. Want a cap for summer? They have numerous. Or a bucket hat? You bet. Oh, they also do decks, if you're looking to update your board.

An afternoon of
vintage shopping

Come the weekend and gaggles of magpie-eyed Manhattanites make pilgrimages across the Brooklyn Bridge, armed with credit cards and trusty totes. Stylish Williamsburg and down-to-earth Greenpoint await on the other side, both bubbling over with weathered emporiums stuffed full of old-school treasures; when it comes to reclaimed fashion, northern Brooklyn is the holy grail. Williamsburg is the place to begin – just be sure to save space in your tote for Greenpoint.

1. Antoinette
119 Grand Street, Williamsburg; www.antoinettebrooklyn.com
///loans.villa.drums

2. Catbird
219 Bedford Avenue, Williamsburg;
www.catbirdnyc.com
///closet.shift.cuts

3. Awoke Vintage
16 Bedford Avenue, Greenpoint;
www.awokevintage.com
///goad.paused.acted

4. Dusty Rose
595 Manhattan Avenue, Greenpoint;
www.dustyrosevintage.com
///soon.ally.milky

5. The Break
41 Norman Avenue, Greenpoint;
www.shopthebreak.com
///mixers.boats.soon

 Sweet Chick
///closet.shift.cuts

Peter Pan Donut and Pastry Shop
///pits.courier.mutual

East River

KENT

Mooch around ANTOINETTE
Start at this cute, simply decorated vintage shop in Williamsburg, where the friendly owner will guide you through their well-curated stock.

1

FRANKLIN STREET

GREENPOINT AVENUE

GREENPOINT

Peter Pan Donut and Pastry Shop *gives true meaning to "retro" – it opened in 1953 and has been serving tasty donuts ever since.*

LORIMER STREET

HUMBOLDT STREET

NORMAN AVE

Stock up at
THE BREAK
Peruse a cool selection of vintage and new clothing, plus jewelry and houseware.

5

Pop into
AWOKE VINTAGE
This Aussie vintage store is becoming a bit of an institution in Greenpoint. Find the used clothes of your vintage dreams hanging from the colorful racks.

3

WYTHE AVE

NASSAU AVE

4

Rifle through
DUSTY ROSE
Looking for something quirky? You may have to dig deep in the clothing and accessory bins at this warehouse but a sharp eye is always rewarded.

Sweet Chick *is co-owned by restaurateur John Seymour and legendary Queens MC, Nas. It's a great spot for Southern soul food.*

McCarren Park

AVENUE

NORTH 7TH STREET

NORTH 10TH STREET

UNION AVENUE

LORIMER STREET

BROOKLYN - QUEENS EXPRESSWAY

BEDFORD

2 Treat yourself at
CATBIRD
Splurge on a piece of jewelry that you literally can't lose at Catbird's (elegant bracelets and necklaces are welded onto you in the store).

GRAND STREET

METROPOLITAN AVENUE

WILLIAMSBURG

| 0 meters | 300 |
| 0 yards | 300 |

ARTS & CULTURE

New York's electric cultural offerings are the backbone of the city. Art, theater, and history are integral to the city's identity, and inspire the changemakers of tomorrow.

City History

This is a gloriously diverse city and New Yorkers are incredibly proud of their shared past. These museums might be small but, boy, are they mighty, and they're great places to start learning.

NEW YORK TRANSIT MUSEUM

Map 5; 99 Schermerhorn Street, Brooklyn Heights, Brooklyn; ///arch.slimy.attend; www.nytransitmuseum.org

While New Yorkers pound the city streets as they go about their daily business, there's another world beneath their feet. It's a world that the New York Transit Museum has captured with hands-on exhibits, based appropriately in an abandoned subway station dating from 1936. It's a fascinating museum and is especially popular with families and young couples hosting their out-of-town friends.

TENEMENT MUSEUM

Map 2; 103 Orchard Street, Lower East Side; ///likes.settle.glory; www.tenement.org

The Lower East Side has a dynamic history of immigration, with newcomers constantly reshaping the neighborhood. This museum tells some of these migrant stories. Energetic and supremely knowledgeable docents shepherd small groups around restored tenement apartments, bringing stories of families and shopkeepers to life. With New Yorkers fiercely proud of their history and ancestry, tour members are just as likely to be locals (of all ages) as tourists eager to hear compelling narratives of the past.

» **Don't leave without** parting with your paycheck in the gift shop, which has an incredible collection of books and classy NYC souvenirs.

THE NEW-YORK HISTORICAL SOCIETY

Map 3; 170 Central Park West, Upper West Side;
///charm.design.regime; www.nyhistory.org

The crowd you'll see here largely depends on the rotating exhibit: fashion students flocked to see the Alexander McQueen display while wannabe wizards came in their droves for a Harry Potter showcase. Ultimately, though, New York's oldest museum is dedicated to the city's, especially Manhattan's, rich cultural history. Its collection includes stunning Tiffany lamps, 19th-century board games, and other treasures that showcase American history in unexpected ways.

Try it!
PHOTOGRAPH HISTORY

While tourists schlep through the halls of Ellis Island, why not book onto a photography tour with Tony Sweet? He'll take you to abandoned areas and help you capture moody photos *(www.tonysweet.com)*.

MUSEUM OF THE CITY OF NEW YORK

Map 3; 1220 Fifth Avenue, Upper East Side; ///wings.sheets.garden;

www.mcny.org

Your parents will *love* this comprehensive museum. The permanent exhibit, "New York at Its Core," outlines 400 years of history, but the Future City Lab is where they can get hands-on and speculate about NYC's future development. The museum also hosts great exhibitions about sport, which often focus on underrepresented stories, like Jackie Robinson's breaking of baseball's color line in the 1940s.

BROOKLYN HISTORICAL SOCIETY

Map 5; 128 Pierrepont Street, Brooklyn Heights, Brooklyn;

///nature.acted.metals; www.brooklynhistory.org

What was a commuter suburb in the 19th century is now (arguably) the coolest of boroughs. And this museum, library, and educational center celebrates Brooklyn's vibrant history and culture. Exhibits aside, there are great lectures, discussions, and film screenings that keep the city's diverse audiences coming back again and again.

MUSEUM OF RECLAIMED URBAN SPACE

Map 2; 155 Loisaida Avenue, Alphabet City; ///chip.lanes.tunes;

www.morusnyc.org

The East Village is famous for its urban activism and this volunteer-run museum celebrates the neighborhood's history of grassroots action. Exhibits include a history of the squatting movement, which saw artists and activists reclaim many of the city's derelict buildings, and emotive

The Christopher Street Tours set off just west from here; they're a great way to learn about LGBTQ+ history. | quilts stitched by the Social Justice Sewing Academy. There's also lots on the city's community gardens, which are vital patches of green in the concrete jungle.

THE CITY RELIQUARY MUSEUM

Map 4; 370 Metropolitan Avenue, Williamsburg, Brooklyn;
///soft.rope.rides; www.cityreliquary.org

Weird? Yes. Missable? No. Grab your friends and head to this nostalgic museum, squeezed between two nondescript restaurants, for truly unique enlightenment. It's a bizarre celebration of the city's past and present, with cultural relics like dentures and exhibits on garbage collection offering a window into the lives of New Yorkers. Museum crowds don't usually make it this far east so you and your pals will feel like you have the tiny treasure all to yourselves.

» Don't leave without asking for the scavenger hunt card pack and compete against your friends to tick off all the listed artifacts.

MUSEUM OF THE AMERICAN GANGSTER

Map 2; 78 St. Mark's Place, Ukrainian Village;
///bottom.atomic.sounds; 212-228-5736

We've all seen *Gangs of New York* and *The Godfather* but when it comes to the genuine history of organized crime in NYC the Museum of the American Gangster is the go-to. And, yeah, it might be tiny but it packs a punch. Based in a former speakeasy, the macabre museum displays bullets from various massacres and gangster death masks.

Favorite Museums

Thanks to their fame, the city's monolithic museums can get crowded – but don't fret. Cool, creative events and often-overlooked institutions mean you don't have to battle the crowds.

AMERICAN MUSEUM OF NATURAL HISTORY

Map 3; 200 Central Park West, Upper West Side; ///idea.nurses.asserts; www.amnh.org

While wide-eyed kids rule the roost during the day, this museum is the domain of adults come nightfall. A curious crowd of young professionals mingle at the Sleepovers for Grown-Ups, getting up close and personal with the exhibits, pairing reds and whites with prehistoric artifacts, and enjoying 3D screenings in the planetarium.

EL MUSEO DEL BARRIO

Map 3; 1230 Fifth Avenue, East Harlem; ///hang.cliff.rises; www.elmuseo.org

This East Harlem institution is more than a museum; it's a hub for Latin American culture. Specializing in Puerto Rican, Caribbean, and Latin American art, it showcases hundreds of years of history, shining an important spotlight on groups who are often under-represented or ignored in mainstream museums. Expect small but powerful rotating exhibits and regular community events, like educational fun runs, salsa socials, and music performances.

THE RUBIN
Map 1; 150 West 17th Street, Chelsea; ///drama.shares.trap; www.rubinmuseum.org

Dedicated to art and culture from Asia's Himalayan region, the impressively curated Rubin somehow flies under the radar. But visitors of all ages soon find themselves drawn into the narrative of its collection, which features Buddhist art and artifacts spanning thousands of years. This is the place to bring the parents and peruse detailed explanation cards that put exhibits into perspective. You'll enter complete novices to Himalayan art and leave as experts.

» **Don't leave without** staying late for K2 Friday Nights, which feature cocktails, live DJ sets, pan-Asian bites, and guided tours with museum curators. Mom and dad will also love it.

Try it!
ARTFUL MEDITATION

Feeling a bit frazzled? The Rubin runs 45-minute meditation classes, with each session inspired by a painting from the museum's collection. So you'll leave with new art knowledge and feeling zen.

THE BROOKLYN MUSEUM

Map 5; 200 Eastern Parkway, Prospect Heights Brooklyn;
///sings.ranks.brush; www.brooklynmuseum.org

There's always an excuse to pop into this Brooklyn stalwart. Family visiting from out of town? Seeking refuge from a downpour? This beloved museum is a hit thanks to its collection of Egyptian and American artifacts. The exhibit locals always come back to? *The Dinner Party*, in the Elizabeth A. Sackler Center for Feminist Art, a feminist work depicting 39 place settings that each represents a woman of note (think Sojourner Truth and Queen Elizabeth I).

THE MORGAN LIBRARY & MUSEUM

Map 3; 225 Madison Avenue, Murray Hill; ///cotton.robot.trend;
www.themorgan.org

Leave the jostling crowds and screaming kids of the Met behind you and head to the often-forgotten Morgan, the private library of banker J.P. Morgan. The pièce de résistance is the East Room,

Shh!

The Brooklyn Public Library (*www.bklynlibrary.org*) hosts various events, including a marathon Night of Philosophy and Ideas, in which leading scholars give lectures. Agreed, it all sounds very intellectual but it's actually tailored for the masses and is accessible to all. Oh, and it's free.

which the financier filled with books he'd amassed during his life. Look closely at the shelves and you'll spot classics like Mary Shelley's *Frankenstein* and works by John Steinbeck and Mark Twain.

COOPER HEWITT SMITHSONIAN DESIGN MUSEUM

Map 3; 2 East 91st Street, Upper East Side; ///hulk.slide.makes; www.cooperhewitt.org

This ornate building, once home to the grandiose Andrew Carnegie Mansion, may give off all the airs of old-world New York but inside it's wholly modern. Light and airy museum galleries are peppered with cool design exhibits, like ultra-trendy mid-century furniture and groovy 3D-printed vases. Want a similarly beautifully designed trinket to take home? You won't leave the gift shop empty-handed.

» Don't leave without exploring the Arthur Ross Terrace and Garden, a serene outdoor space that's updated regularly with design pieces.

THE WHITNEY MUSEUM OF AMERICAN ART

Map 1; 99 Gansevoort Street, Meatpacking District; ///hurry.stick.edge; www.whitney.org

Founded by the formidable Gertrude Vanderbilt Whitney, in 1931, this museum has seen many resurrections. Now standing by the Hudson, it draws an artsy crowd looking for provocative art that's made in the USA. The biggest event on the calendar? It's got to be the Whitney Biennial (in 2022, 2024, 2026 – you get the picture).

Art Spaces

Never ones to follow the crowd, New Yorkers love to push the boundaries and express themselves through art. Whether paintings, installations, or living art, works are displayed in the most inclusive spaces.

CANADA

Map 1; 60 Lispenard Street, Tribeca; ///sounds.stays.trap; www.canadanewyork.com

Four artists sought to create a gallery that displayed the kind of art that they loved: unconventional, groundbreaking, and with community at the forefront. And so Canada was born. A talent incubator since the 90s, the gallery and its artworks are diverse, to say the least; you'll find hipsters stroking their beards in front of subversive, political exhibits just as easily as art historians swooning over whimsical paintings.

FIVEMYLES

Map 5; 558 St. Johns Place, Crown Heights, Brooklyn; ///engage.mint.views; www.fivemyles.org

Travelers that venture as far as Crown Heights will be rewarded with this exciting gallery space – a gem that would draw bigger crowds, if only they knew about it. The gallery prioritizes works by underrepresented, experimental artists of various mediums, especially those from non-Western cultures. It's a space where art and community connect, sometimes even on the sidewalk outside.

>> Don't leave without donating, even if it's just a few dollars, which will go towards supporting budding artists looking to showcase their work.

AMORPHIC ROBOT WORKS

Map 5; 111 Pioneer Street, Red Hook, Brooklyn; ///rises.itself.drag; www.amorphicrobotworks.org

Ever seen an orchestra of robots play in an abandoned church? In the former Norwegian Seaman's Church you'll find just that, with machinery brought to life thanks to the magic touch of artist Chico MacMurtrie. The Robotic Church's mechanical musicians – which scrape across the floor and crawl across the ceiling like phantoms in a horror movie – are a sight to behold.

IVY BROWN GALLERY

Map 1; 675 Hudson Street, Meatpacking District; ///took.spit.coherent; www.ivybrowngallery.org

Collectors don't get much cooler than art trailblazer and pioneer Ivy Brown. She moved to the Meatpacking District in the 80s, then a neighborhood that others dared not set foot in, and transformed her fourth-floor apartment into her own private contemporary art gallery. When the Twin Towers fell, in 2001, Brown felt that her fellow New Yorkers needed art for solace, and so she threw her doors open to the public. She hasn't closed them since.

# THE STUDIO MUSEUM IN HARLEM
Map 6; 144 West 125th Street, Harlem; ///hurray.fakes.hung;
www.studiomuseum.org

This too-often-overlooked art museum is all about showcasing the works of artists of African descent, including artists-in-residence. Displaying paintings, drawings, sculptures, watercolors, and mixed-media installations, the space is a major promoter of Afrofuturism art and events celebrating Black Americans. It's a must-visit.

» Don't leave without taking a free Harlem postcard made by a contemporary artist – the perfect addition to your living room wall.

# ARTISTS SPACE
Map 1; 11 Cortlandt Alley, Tribeca; ///terms.flank.drum;
www.artistsspace.org

Hell, the art world is a cutthroat one, so thank heavens for the Artists Space. This nonprofit gallery is a refuge for noncommercial artists, giving them pure freedom of expression, and likewise attracts freethinkers wanting to stretch their minds with conceptual art.

# THE KITCHEN
Map 3; 512 West 19th Street, Chelsea; ///cakes.deaf.agree;
www.thekitchen.org

The Kitchen has been cooking up an artistic storm since the 1970s. Supporting and showcasing emerging artists, the nonprofit displays painting and sculpture, plus avant-garde living art in its black box theater. This is the place to discover the next big name in the art world.

Liked by the locals

"Smaller art spaces bring communities together and celebrate the things that they share in common. It was NYC's indie galleries that welcomed me with fresh white walls, support, and warmth – and gave me the confidence to keep creating."

PIA SAWHNEY, CONTEMPORARY ARTIST AND MUSICIAN

Street Art

Nowhere else does street art like NYC. And anything goes as a canvas here – alleyways, restaurant facades, subway stations. You name it, and there's probably a tagger working on it.

FIRST STREET GREEN CULTURAL PARK

**Map 2; 33 East 1st Street, Lower East Side; ///zone.rigid.pads;
www.firststreetgreenpark.org**

A derelict building lot turned urban park, First Street Green is one of the best spots to catch art in the making, with walls evolving from each day to the next. Not only that, but the space also hosts performances and workshops – all with a colorful backdrop of street art.

THE BUSHWICK COLLECTIVE

**Map 4; 427 Troutman Street, Bushwick, Brooklyn; ///hello.wedge.slices;
www.thebushwickcollective.com**

Take the L train to Jefferson Street to explore the largest continuous collection of street art in America. The Bushwick Collective began as a charity fundraiser, with businesses offering their walls to artists, and visitors paying a sum to see the artworks. Arrive with your camera and posse, and stick around for the long haul, winding your way

Weary feet? Rest up with a drink at nearby Brooklyn Beer Garden, which is decorated with more urban art.

through warehouses and past restaurants adorned with changing works by street artists from across the world. There are laods of places to stop for refreshment.

FREEMAN ALLEY

Map 2; Freeman Alley, Lower East Side; ///tend.rated.laptop

Teenagers flock to inconspicuous Freeman Alley, which harbors challenging and politicized art. The neighborhood around it might have gentrified, with an influx of upscale coffee shops frequented by hipsters, but this dead-end alley captures the area's raw, grittier spirit, with a mishmash of ever-changing pieces by relative newcomers, like PhoebeNewYork and Jappy Agoncillo.

» **Don't leave without** popping into Freemans while you're here. It's an unmarked restaurant decorated like an old rustic tavern.

BOWERY MURAL

Map 1; 76 East Houston Street, Lower East Side; ///means.rigid.them

Once upon a time, legendary graffiti artist Keith Haring painted a mural on a wall on the corner of Bowery and Houston. The year was 1982. Fast forward to what would have been Haring's 50th birthday, in 2008, and the wall was officially earmarked for the use of street artists to create public artworks. And so an icon of urban art was born. Every year a new mural appears; 2020 saw Ecuadorean Raul Ayala create an emotive composition around Black Lives Matter that captured his hope for a unified, peaceful future in spray paint.

THE AUDUBON MURAL PROJECT

Map 6; 149th Street and Broadway, Washington Heights;
///dollar.skills.junior; www.audubon.org

Traipse around West Harlem and you'll spot a whole horde of bird-themed murals. This is no coincidence; this is the Audubon Mural Project, which aims to highlight the impact that climate change has on our feathered friends with street art. Download a map online to locate the 80 or so murals (the biggest group is on Broadway).

TUNNEL STREET

Map 6; 191 St Subway Station, Broadway, Washington Heights;
///armed.pest.loved

You'll likely be confused when you arrive at Tunnel Street. Yes, this is in fact a subway station; 191 St Station, to be precise. Enter the station's colorful archway and walk along the passageway, where

Shh!

It's hard to ignore the colorful entrance of 191 St Subway but there's actually more art beneath the city streets. Underground subway stations have been decorated with masterpieces commissioned to beautify these shabby spaces.

At the 86th St Q stop, 12 enormous Chuck Close photo-based mosaics shimmer in their abstract glory, while at 23rd St F and M stops, William Wegman has created mosaic portraits of dogs dressed up in flannel and raincoats.

900 ft (275 m) of murals have transformed a previously dank stretch of grubby yellow wall. Now psychedelic designs, pop art, and motivational messages by a diverse group of taggers pump up commuting office workers and college students for the day ahead.

DUMBO WALLS

Map 5; Brooklyn Queens Expressway, Dumbo, Brooklyn;
///land.think.entertainer

Spanning four blocks along the Brooklyn Queens Expressway, Dumbo's murals are creative and varied, just like the artists who have made the neighborhood their home. Grab a coffee from TimeOut Market *(p46)* and explore: walk along the Jay Street Underpass where Japanese illustrator Yuko Shimizu's octopus wades through ocean waves; stroll to York and Jay streets to see Shepard Fairey's nouveau-style woman who represents peace; and end up at Prospect and Jay streets, home to satisfyingly symmetrical shapes by French artist Eltono.

GRAFFITI HALL OF FAME

Map 3; Park Avenue, Harlem; ///voters.rent.milky

Back in the 1980s, activist Ray Rodriguez believed graffiti was a safe way for kids to tell their stories and celebrate hip-hop culture. So he acquired a derelict schoolyard and made it into a sanctioned space for artists to practice their skills, giving birth to the Graffiti Hall of Fame. Today a cool crowd of taggers continue to leave their mark.

» **Don't leave without** heading to the nearby Spirit of East Harlem, a permanent, four-story mural that depicts neighborhood residents.

Off-Broadway

While the blinding lights of Times Square often steal the spotlight for out-of-towners, locals usually turn to off-Broadway theater for ovation-worthy perform-ances, top-notch playwrights, and cheaper prices.

SIGNATURE THEATRE COMPANY

Map 3; 480 West 42nd Street, Hell's Kitchen; ///agent.upset.chimp; www.signaturetheatre.org

Signature is an absolute powerhouse. The Hell's Kitchen company produces showstopping new works and revivals, but what makes it so special is the "Residence" program, where the company focuses on fostering talent by showcasing several shows by the same playwright across five years. Seats for the first five weeks of every show are just $35, which makes it a hit with students.

ST. ANN'S WAREHOUSE

Map 5; 45 Water Street, Dumbo, Brooklyn; ///moved.comic.status; www.stannswarehouse.org

Housed in what used to be a 19th-century tobacco warehouse, this gorgeous waterfront theater is known as a hub for avant-garde works, which naturally attracts freethinkers like moths to a flame.

A shapeshifter, the roomy space can be transformed to fit any purpose, so all manner of productions, from reimagined Shakespeare classics to multi-artist shows, take place beneath its soaring ceilings.

» Don't leave without strolling around Brooklyn Bridge Park at sunset before your show starts for dramatic East River and Manhattan views.

LA MAMA EXPERIMENTAL THEATRE CLUB

Map 2; 66 East 4th Street, East Village; ///cook.roofs.large; www.lamama.org

Looking for a date night with a difference? Head to this place, one of the original "off-off-Broadway" companies. Set up in the 60s by NYC theater legend Ellen Stewart, who would choose a script based on the feeling it gave her rather than the actual script itself, La MaMa is dedicated to taking risks – just like its founder. It stages brave, bold shows that push the boundaries, so it follows that radicals, students, and general theater-fanatics are regulars here.

NEW YORK THEATRE WORKSHOP

Map 2; 79 East 4th Street, East Village; ///tamed.worth.punchy; www.nytw.org

Jonathan Larson, Caryl Churchill, and Tony Kushner have all seen their works produced at NYTW, including Larson's classic *Rent*, which first debuted here. But for such a big-hitting theater space, this intimate nonprofit was actually made for artists to create outside of the confines of commercially driven theater. The result is exciting and surprising productions in a cozy – if slightly fraying – space.

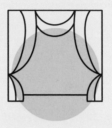

Liked by the locals

"Every time I leave a New York theater I wonder why I don't go more often. It sheds away every weight and awful thing, and makes you fall in love with the city all around you."

SEAN MURPHY, PLAYWRIGHT AND ACTOR

BAM HARVEY THEATER

Map 5; 651 Fulton Street, Fort Greene, Brooklyn;
///bolt.handed.much; www.bam.org

The Majestic Theater was a beacon in Brooklyn's early entertainment era thanks to its progressive productions that challenged views of the time. Revived by devoted patrons and renamed the Harvey, today the theater attracts a young, cool audience of Brooklynites. Shows range from modern pan-African stories to revisited classic plays.

THE PUBLIC THEATER

Map 1; 425 Lafayette Street, Noho;
///leaned.salads.tiny; www.publictheater.org

Your parents are visiting, quick, book tickets to the Public! Once the stage for the 1967 musical *HAIR*, this is also where a talented cast rose a glass to freedom after the now-legendary *Hamilton* premiered in 2015. The Public is even behind the beloved Shakespeare in the Park. Join an excited audience, sit back, and prepare to be entertained.

» Don't leave without checking out Joe's Pub, a venue in the Public that hosts everything from drag cabaret to international bands.

SOHO REPERTORY THEATRE

Map 1; 46 Walker Street, Tribeca; ///tall.damp.vocal; www.sohorep.org

Although this 73-seat venue might be small (cozy, if you will), it's known as an effervescent hub for radical theater. The productions at "Soho Rep.", as locals call it, often defy the traditional boundaries of theater, challenging audiences with raw acting and difficult subject matters.

Movie Theaters

In a city with a movie backdrop at every turn, it's no wonder there's a hardcore cadre of cinephiles here. Join them at their favorite arthouse theaters, which proudly guard the city's cinematic tradition.

THE IFC CENTER

Map 1; 323 Sixth Avenue, West Village; ///sticks.turned.calms; www.ifccenter.com

This bare-bones cinema feels a bit like someone's personal screening room, with some of the theaters only housing 32 seats. It's a gathering spot for serious film buffs, with a studious hush enveloping the theater once the reel starts playing – a far cry from the thrum of whispering and texting that plagues many commercial theaters. Expect an array of arthouse films, as well as documentaries and throwback movies.

THE PARIS THEATER

Map 3; 4 West 58th Street, Midtown; ///rank.work.coach; www.paristheaternyc.com

Like it's been plucked from the grand age of cinema, this movie theater is a beauty. It's also Manhattan's last single-screen, with a whopping 571 seats. The Paris Theater has been on a hell of an adventure since Marlene Dietrich cut the ribbon at its opening in 1948, going on to screen arthouse and foreign-language films that drew intellectuals and creatives. Alas the cinema closed in 2019, before Netflix swooped in and saved the space from ruin, and now the Paris Theater an impressive place for the streaming platform to showcase some of its best work.

METROGRAPH

Map 2; 7 Ludlow Street, Lower East Side;
///page.easy.badly; www.metrograph.com

This isn't your average cinema. Metrograph popped up in 2016 and quickly became a cultural nucleus for New York's movie lovers. Groups of 20- and 30-somethings spend whole days in the complex – catching a movie, browsing the bookstore, and dining in the lovely restaurant. With its Art Deco-inspired branding and dynamic events lineup, it's a pretty cool spot, with a pretty cool crowd.

>> Don't leave without sipping on cocktails in Metrograph Commissary, the complex's restaurant, decorated like a 1920s Hollywood canteen.

Need inspiration for a date? Bushwick's Syndicated Bar Theater Kitchen has a retro cinema, though true romantics might prefer to stay in the bar area, where old and classic movies are projected onto the wall *(www.syndicatedbk.com)*.

NITEHAWK CINEMA

Map 4; 136 Metropolitan Avenue, Williamsburg, Brooklyn;
///pass.twice.engine; www.nitehawkcinema.com

Why settle for just a movie when you can have dinner and a show? Nitehawk offers a full menu of global food and drink – we're talking fish tacos, tater tots, tuna wontons – so you can booze and snack as you enjoy your movie. Check out the upstairs retro-style bar if you want to keep the party going, and look out for the midnight showings.

SPECTACLE THEATER

Map 4; 124 South 3rd Street, Williamsburg, Brooklyn;
///torn.jets.exam; www.spectacletheater.com

Tucked away Spectacle is a collectively run cinema showing obscure and ultra-indie works. Its owners, volunteers, and audiences clearly love films, and heartily embrace the oddball and radical features. Entry is only $5 for regular showings and $10 for special events, with a BYOB and BYO-food policy. (Caveat: it's a teeny-tiny space, the kind where a whisper ricochets like a scream, so excessive chewing will ignite fury.)

VILLAGE EAST CINEMA

Map 2; 181–189 Second Avenue, East Village; ///scam.noting.clip;
www.citycinemas.com

Built in the 1920s, this theater was the vibrant epicenter for Yiddish-language comedies and musicals. The building itself is stunning, with intricate design details found where you least expect them. Beside from being historically important and beautifully designed,

Village East is also known for its roster of film festivals; you'll be able to tell when they're hosting one by the excited line of movie nerds outside. After a classic indie flick? Prefer blockbusters to arthouse movies? Good news: Village East screens these, too.

» Don't leave without looking up at the cinema's main auditorium ceiling, a gorgeous, ornate masterpiece of gold and plaster workmanship.

FILM FORUM
Map 1; 209 West Houston Street, West Village;
///entry.range.tree; www.filmforum.org

Standing stalwart in the Village, this nonprofit movie theater has an impeccably curated selection of indie, foreign, and classic films (some of which you'd be hard pressed to find anywhere else). The clientele, like the staff, are largely film aficionados, who crowd in on the weekend to experience one of NYC's last-standing arthouse theaters. Although the owners renovated the space in 2018 and made seating a smidge roomier, it's still quite basic – but nobody's here for the luxe setup.

ANGELIKA FILM CENTER
Map 1; 18 West Houston Street, Greenwich Village;
///sheets.pasta.hush; www.angelikafilmcenter.com;

In the beaux-arts Cable Building, the Angelika recreates a bit of old-world glamor and showcases a consistently good lineup of indie and foreign films. Once through the blazing neon entrance, be sure to follow the laid-back patrons to the café, where you can stock up on tasty pre-film pastries from Sacred Chow, a local vegan restaurant.

EAST
WILLIAMSBURG

**Fuel up at
ROBERTA'S**

Wolf down a slice of pizza
from this hipster hangout
before checking out
the parking lot where
Mission Graffiti, or the
MG Boys, like to tag.

*A few months before the
2020 election, a local
community radio station
created a colorful **Wall
of Lies** told by President
Trump while in office.*

**Sip a beer at
KINGS COUNTRY
BREWERS COLLECTIVE**

Time for a reviving bev? Draw
up a stool in this taproom and,
while you drink, admire the beer
cans' graffiti-style labels.

JOHNSON

AVENUE

THAMES   ST

1

2

**Admire the works along
VANDERVOORT PLACE**

Don't be fooled into thinking this
is a regular side street. Stroll down
for constantly changing artworks;
the paint might still be drying.

BOGART   ST

FLUSHING   AVENUE

WILSON

AVENUE

STREET

STREET

TROUTMAN

STREET

KNICKERBOCKER

*Maria
Hernandez
Park*

3

4

**Get snapping on
TROUTMAN
STREET**

A veritable treasure trove
of art, Troutman offers
mural after mural. Take
your time wandering
down, and stop for
obligatory photos.

EVERGREEN

AVENUE

NOLL

GEORGE

STREET

BUSHWICK

CENTRAL

AVENUE

0 meters   250
0 yards   250

MYRTLE   AVENUE

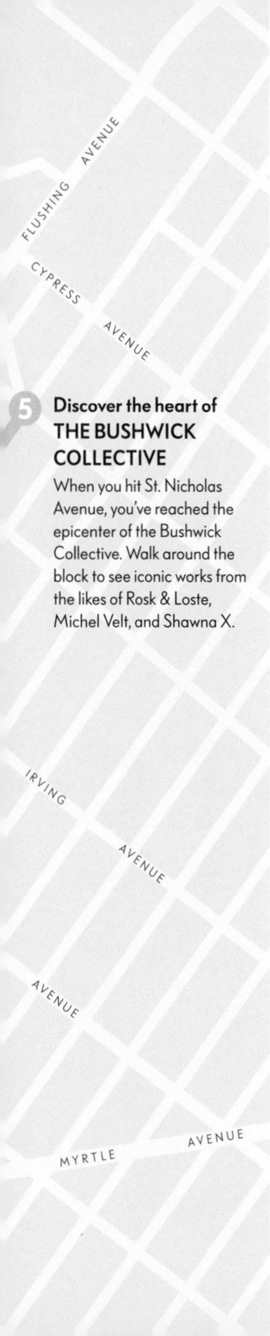

An afternoon in
arty Bushwick

Williamsburg not edgy enough for you? Amble east to Bushwick, a less-explored enclave and mecca for street art. As rents have risen across Brooklyn, artists and creatives have moved to this former industrial area and transformed it into a vibrant cityscape that celebrates the local community. Ease your stride and seek out the constantly changing open-air gallery of the Bushwick Collective *(p124)*.

5 **Discover the heart of THE BUSHWICK COLLECTIVE**
When you hit St. Nicholas Avenue, you've reached the epicenter of the Bushwick Collective. Walk around the block to see iconic works from the likes of Rosk & Loste, Michel Velt, and Shawna X.

1. Roberta's
261 Moore Street, Williamsburg; www.robertaspizza.com
///settle.took.photo

2. Vandervoort Place
Vandervoort Place, Williamsburg;
///fumes.reap.candy

3. Troutman Street
Troutman Street, Bushwick
///skills.really.trials

4. Kings Country Brewers Collective
381 Troutman Street, Bushwick;
www.kcbcbeer.com
///dared.major.sides

5. The Bushwick Collective
Troutman Street and St. Nicholas Avenue, Bushwick; www.thebushwickcollective.com
///hello.wedge.slices

📍 **Wall of Lies** ///later.trunk.recall

Map labels: FLUSHING AVENUE, CYPRESS AVENUE, IRVING AVENUE, AVENUE, MYRTLE AVENUE

NIGHTLIFE

There's truth to the saying that this city never sleeps. NYC has a different persona when the sun sets; a network of venues unfurl and find new life in the thrum of the night.

Comedy Nights

When friends from out of town are visiting, New Yorkers book tickets for a night of comedy. After all, this city has produced some of the best comics out there. And they started on these stages.

MAGNET THEATER

Map 3; 254 West 29th Street, Chelsea; ///fried.them.alien; www.magnettheater.com

Silliness abounds at the Magnet Theater, a hub of nightly improv and sketch comedy. Just like its down-to-earth audience, the theater is known for attracting ego-free performers who just want to entertain. The space itself is simple and small, so when that lady in the front row giggles uncontrollably, you can't help but join in.

Try it!
AN INTRO TO IMPROV

Feeling brave? The PIT in Midtown offers $20 drop-in sessions, where you'll learn the basics of improv and eschew your inhibitions with a group of new friends (*www.thepit-nyc.com*).

Performances are raucous but especially the Tuesday and Wednesday all-nighter "Megawatt" gigs, during which a single ticket permits access to each hour-long improv performance.

VILLAGE UNDERGROUND

Map 1; 117 MacDougal Street, Greenwich Village; ///sushi.smiled.slides; www.comedycellar.com

Headliners embody the essence of New York comedy – scrappy, vulgar, surprising – at this, the slightly roomier (legroom, hallelujah) sister of the iconic Comedy Cellar *(p142)*. The lineup is still top-notch, with talent ping-ponged between the two venues, and performances provoke similar gasping-for-air laughter. It's easier to grab tickets here, but don't sleep on reserving for either location.

GOTHAM COMEDY CLUB

Map 3; 208 West 23rd Street, Chelsea; ///drove.squad.usual; www.gothamcomedyclub.com

Those who like their comedy with a dollop of sophistication book a spot at Gotham Comedy Club, which is inspired by the 1920s nightclub "look" complete with intimate tables – perfect for date night. And the comedy ethos reflects the classy setting here. It's all about mutual respect between the comic and their audience, so you can rest assured that you'll be howling with laughter without the fear of being picked on.

» **Don't leave without** stopping to study the photographs of comics on the entry walls (look in particular for comedy legend Robin Williams).

THE BELL HOUSE

Map 5; 149 7th Street, Gowanus, Brooklyn; ///good.wide.chop;
www.thebellhouseny.com

A quirky audience, who prefer their comedy to be less mainstream and more wild, shuffle into the Bell House. And they're never disappointed. The venue hosts eye-wateringly funny stand-up and podcast recordings, plus live music performances for good measure. It's standing room only so get there early and stake out your spot.

BROOKLYN HOUSE OF COMEDY

Map 4; 211 Putnam Avenue, Bed-Stuy, Brooklyn;
///outfit.dirt.blend; 718-926-0091

Is there anything more thrilling than discovering a diamond that's still managed to fly under the radar? Take the Black-owned Brooklyn House of Comedy, which consistently features hilarious local acts and promotes Black comedians. The audience is diverse, made up of longtime Bed-Stuy residents who hobnob with young professional transplants, all united in spilling their drinks as they chuckle at Brooklyn's best budding comics. You'll thank us for the tip-off.

COMEDY CELLAR

Map 1; 117 MacDougal Street, Greenwich Village; ///flip.lance.broad;
www.comedycellar.com

The Village has no shortage of comedy clubs in its ranks but this is the cream of the crop. Dozens of comics work their way onto the stage each night, like a tag team of professional heavyweights. This is where you'll see the next big act practice their craft or – if you're really lucky – a celebrity comic like Dave Attell, Jerry Seinfeld, Dave Chappelle, Aziz Ansari, Amy Schumer, or Chris Rock (an actual Wednesday-night lineup in 2017). This is one for the planners, who book ahead to enjoy a night of laugh-until-you-feel-sick comedy.

» Don't leave without chowing down on a meal here – the food is surprisingly good for an entertainment venue.

STAND UP NY

Map 3; 236 West 78th Street, Upper West Side; ///breed.slave.statue;
www.standupny.com

A favorite with college students and office workers, Stand Up NY is smaller than many of its comedy counterparts but, boy, does it pack a punch. It's itty-bitty, with a shorter line for entry, and comics here tend to rely on a lot of crowd work. So if you want to be part of the joke, bag a seat front and center.

LITTLEFIELD

Map 5; 635 Sackett Street, Gowanus, Brooklyn; ///dream.laser.state;
www.littlefieldnyc.com

Though Littlefield isn't exclusively a comedy venue (it also hosts live music, podcast recordings, and film screenings), the programing is consistently hilarious. It's a home away from home for many up-and-coming comedians testing out their material, and the audience often comprises their friends and families cheering on in support. Add in die-hard comedy fans and you've got an electric night out.

Culture Live

The city has long attracted artists, writers, comics, musicians, and intellectuals looking to tell their story on a public stage. These places of refuge are where all walks of life come together, and all voices are heard.

92ND STREET Y

Map 3; 1395 Lexington Avenue, Upper East Side; ///coins.ideal.tell; www.92y.org

It might be a schlep uptown but this cultural powerhouse is worth it. Why? Well, the lineup of concerts, interviews, and talks is incredible. An "average" week might feature Malcolm Gladwell in conversation with Ezra Klein, an event with Zadie Smith, and a jazz band to top it off.

BOWERY POETRY CLUB

Map 1; 308 Bowery, East Village; ///loving.aside.tiger; www.bowerypoetry.com

A hush of quiet sweeps across the crowd at this cute, candlelit venue when a poet stands to perform. It doesn't matter if the verse-slinger is a novice or established, whether they're reading from their phone, a scrap of paper, or are accompanied by a guitar – the vibe is electric. Draw up a chair, pour a glass of wine, and get ready to feel all the feels.

THE TANK

Map 3; 312 West 36th Street, Midtown; ///opera.shirt.lies;
www.thetanknyc.org

Anything goes on the stage at nonprofit The Tank, from eccentric improv shows and experimental theater, to low-budget (or no-budget) film screenings. The audience is usually made up of a supportive group of friends, and friends of friends, and *their* friends, who have somehow been drawn into The Tank's irresistibly kooky web.

» Don't leave without seeing the very fun Rule of 7x7 (monthly), where 7 writers each create a 10-minute play, following the same 7 "rules."

THE PUNDERDOME

Map 5; 635 Sackett Street, Gowanus, Brooklyn; ///pens.mute.motor;
www.littlefieldnyc.com

Hosted by a comedian and her impersonator father, this hilarious Thursday pun-off sees 18 audience members compete with wordplay. It's side-splitting and cringe-worthy all at once. The Human Clap-O-Meter determines who is the winning pun-dit.

CENTER FOR FICTION

Map 5; 15 Lafayette Avenue, Fort Greene, Brooklyn;
///mirror.mock.spout; www.centerforfiction.org

A writer's studio, event space, and bar – oh my! There's nowhere else like this nonprofit, which is all about celebrating fiction. The space is a manifestation of a bookworm's brain, with floor-to-ceiling bookshelves, but the events are the real draw, with talks from various literary voices.

NUYORICAN POETS CAFE

Map 2; 236 East 3rd Street, Alphabet City; ///desks.looks.cake; www.nuyorican.org

The beating heart of the New York Puerto Rican (hence "Nuyorican") community since 1973, this café is as welcoming as they come. A diverse and energetic audience hang on the every word of poets, nod their heads at Jazz Jams, and cheer on hip-hop freestylers.

» Don't leave without having a go at performing something yourself at the Monday night Open Mic night.

CAVEAT

Map 2; 21A Clinton Street, Lower East Side; ///prop.saving.modes; www.caveat.nyc

Friends spread the gospel about this geeky venue with a mix of excitement and reluctance, wanting to both scream about it from the rooftops and keep schtum. Caveat excels at cerebral comedy, staging whip-smart shows that delve into history, science, and current affairs.

SCHOMBURG CENTER FOR RESEARCH IN BLACK CULTURE

Map 6; 515 Malcolm X Boulevard, Harlem; ///likes.motor.softly; www.nypl.org

This sanctuary for literature, artifacts, and events dedicated to Black culture also hosts a dynamic program of lectures, screenings, and guest panels. Our top tip: check out First Fridays, where a crowd of all ages and backgrounds dance, eat, and mingle.

Liked by the locals

"The Schomburg Center's programs reflect the immense Black imagination illustrated in literature, performance, the visual arts, and more. Visitors can expect to experience a range of human emotions and learn comfortable and uncomfortable truths."

NOVELLA FORD, ASSOCIATE DIRECTOR, PUBLIC PROGRAMS & EXHIBITIONS, SCHOMBURG CENTER FOR RESEARCH IN BLACK CULTURE

Live Music

People from all walks of life gather in New York's live music venues, all looking to be carried away by the city's musicians. And with everything from jazz to rock 'n' roll, there's a show for every night of the week.

BOWERY ELECTRIC

Map 2; 327 Bowery, East Village; ///trunk.richer.fend; www.theboweryelectric.com

Follow the young crowd to this East Village spot for some good ol' rock 'n' roll. Serious indie fans in beanies gravitate toward the live bands on the first floor, while pretty young things wanting less live and more jive head down to the basement to dance under the disco ball.

MUSIC HALL OF WILLIAMSBURG

Map 4; 66 North 6th Street, Williamsburg, Brooklyn; ///bunks.penny.yard; www.musichallofwilliamsburg.com

There's a lovely feeling of oldy-worldy NYC at this Brooklyn music hall. Sure, it might be a little frayed around the edges but the set list is stellar, with the main ballroom stage welcoming both indie artists on a meteoric rise and music veterans. For the cool crowd of spectators it's standing room only, but there's enough room to dance.

LUNÁTICO

Map 4; 486 Halsey Street, Bed-Stuy, Brooklyn;
///think.lows.matter; www.barlunatico.com

The three musicians behind Lunático have brought a little slice of the Med to Bed-Stuy, with dollops of India, Africa, and Latin America on top. Cocktails and Mediterranean small plates are paired with flavorful music – we're talking gypsy jazz, Southern swamp rock, and traditional Nigerian Yoruba music – that keeps locals coming time after time.

» Don't leave without sampling the Mrs. Robinson cocktail – a mixture of Earl Grey-infused gin, honey, and lemon. Mrs. Robinson, here's to you.

CLOVER CLUB

Map 5; 210 Smith Street, Cobble Hill, Brooklyn; ///views.rent.juror
www.cloverclubny.com

You can't visit the Big Apple and *not* see live jazz. Brooklyn's answer to Manhattan's clubs is this cocktail bar-turned-jazz joint, the perfect place to impress the parents. Make like you're Gatsby and embrace your inner sophisticant with oysters and crooning music.

Shh!

Let's just keep this between us, deal? In a Harlem townhouse, saxophonist Bill Saxton hosts live jazz and stories of NYC on weekends with an audience of 20 *(www.billsplaceharlem.com)*. He doesn't sell booze, but guests are welcome to bring their own.

Solo, Pair, Crowd

This is a city that never sleeps, remember. So, whoever you're with, NYC promises a night to remember.

FLYING SOLO

All that jazz

Tap your foot to some swinging jazz at the Rum House, in Times Square. It may be in a touristy area but this cozy bar is a great place to meet like-minded people (if you like rum and a party).

IN A PAIR

Groovy gig for two

Swing by Wild Birds in Crown Heights for an intimate date night. With bands playing the infectious beats of rocksteady, bolero, chica, and funk, you'll be dancing until the early hours – trust us.

IN A CROWD

Mercury in retro-great

Craving an all-night party with the gang? Book tickets to the Mercury Lounge, which has hosted touring indie artists since the 90s. It'll be a night you won't forget.

BLUE NOTE

Map 1; 131 West 3rd Street, Greenwich Village; ///rocky.tolls.memory;
www.bluenotejazz.com

As any and every local will tell you, a night at Blue Note is never a bad idea. The traditional music club has an unmatched cadre of performers in the spirit of jazz, blues, folk, and many modern genres inspired by all three. Book ahead; while you can be sure that the music is top drawer, the seats are a crapshoot if you leave them to chance.

ROCKWOOD MUSIC HALL

Map 2; 196 Allen Street, Lower East Side; ///discouraged.entry.hurt;
www.rockwoodmusichall.com

Smack in the Lower East Side is this tiny music venue, where New Yorker Lady Gaga started her career. And when we say tiny, we mean it; it's so intimate, and the vibes are so good, that you'll be dancing with your neighbor before you know it.

DIZZY'S CLUB

Map 3; 10 Columbus Circle, Columbus Circle;
///acted.petal.image; www.jazz.org

When New Yorkers want to feel fancy, they book a spot at the Lincoln Center's Dizzy's Club for a night of classy jazz and Southern cuisine, all framed by the backdrop of Columbus Circle. Sets are at 7:30pm and 9:30pm nightly, with late-night jams Tuesday through Saturday.

» Don't leave without first paying homage to all the jazz greats at the National Jazz Museum in Harlem.

Game Night

Sure, your friends are getting hitched and moving upstate. But just because you're all grown up doesn't mean the fun should stop. Let your hair down with a competitive night of fun and games.

GOTHAM ARCHERY

Map 5; 480 Baltic Street, Gowanus, Brooklyn; ///grew.pushes.puns; www.got-archery.com

Young New Yorkers have realized that they don't need summer camp to fulfill all of their outdoorsy dreams. Groups of wannabe Robin Hoods and Katniss Everdeens make for this facility, where wonderfully patient instructors guide them on becoming sharp-shooters (they also have hatchet- and knife-throwing classes. Gulp).

ACE BAR

Map 2; 531 East 5th Street, Alphabet City; ///towns.exist.last; www.acebar.com

This Alphabet City dive bar is one of those watering holes that serves nearly any purpose: impress a date with your gaming ability, hang with friends on a Friday night, or just return to your younger glory years when being a Skee-Ball champ was the coolest accolade.

A few doors down is Sophie's – one of the 'hood's oldest bars – where you'll find a pool table and jukebox.

Ace Bar offers up pool, darts, and the aforementioned Skee-Ball, as well as lively trivia nights. Take advantage of the cheap drinks to fuel your gameplay.

SUNSHINE LAUNDROMAT

Map 4; 860 Manhattan Avenue, Greenpoint, Brooklyn; ///mats.sprint.dart; www.sunshinelaundromat.com

Tucked behind an actual, functioning laundromat – and accessed by a fake washer/dryer door, no less – is this grungy game bar. Here you and your friends will discover an impressive collection of 30 pinball machines plus traditional board games. Challenge your gang to a tournament and let the winner treat everyone to a round of beers. Or they can go next door and wash all your dirty clothes.

» **Don't leave without** heading to nearby Brooklyn Safehouse, a dive bar with cheap beer and free pool.

BARCADE

Map 3; 148 West 24th Street, Chelsea; ///folds.scale.warm; www.barcadenewyork.com

If beer plus Pac-man is your happy place, make like a hipster and head to Barcade. Here groups of NYU students gather around retro consoles and arcade games, tapping furiously and generally going square-eyed as they challenge others to rounds of Donkey Kong and pinball. It's the number one place for a few hours of addictive gaming – all in the name of nostalgia. Oh, and whoever loses buys the beers.

Liked by the locals

"It's a bit of a trek to get to Royal Palms Shuffleboard, but it's a Gowanus staple. The bar radiates vintage Palm Beach, Fl., vibes with plastic flamingos and tropical drinks. Add a rousing game (or three) of shuffleboard with friends and drinks and things are bound to get exciting."

LIZZY ROSENBERG, WRITER AND EDITOR

THE UNCOMMONS

**Map 1; 230 Thompson Street, Greenwich Village; ///skins.frame.beans;
www.uncommonsnyc.com**

Remember the innocent days of Battleship, Yahtzee, Scrabble, and all those wholesome games that brought you and your family together after school? Hang out in this chock-a-block board game café and revisit a simpler age – this time round with a coffee or beer. Be warned, though: The Uncommons does get busy, with groups of 20- and 30-somethings competing fervently between the piles and piles of games that are stacked to the venue's ceiling. There's a three-hour time limit (and a $10 charge per person) so if you want to continue the board game tournament later, the café also has a shop stocking every game under the sun.

» Don't leave without popping into the Chess Forum next door, a game store with an incredible selection of chess sets, both new and old, from around the world. Head to the back for gameplay.

ROYAL PALMS SHUFFLEBOARD

**Map 5; 514 Union Street, Gowanus, Brooklyn; ///privately.lights.strike;
www.royalpalmsbrooklyn.com**

This one is all about embracing your inner retiree because grandparents like to play games too, you know. Royal Palms really does take shuffleboard *very* seriously; it hosts leagues with nationally ranked teams. But don't worry if you're a beginner, you'll still have an awesome time. Grab your friends (so long as you're in multiples of two), don your jazziest garb for the photo booth, and learn why your grandpa has long been obsessed with shuffleboard.

Cool Clubs

*For all its crowded clubs with expensive drinks and
obnoxious doormen, New York has countless places
to party, make new friends, see world-class DJs and
musicians, and dance until dawn.*

DREAM BABY

**Map 2; 162–164 Avenue B, Alphabet City; ///factor.slips.sweat;
www.dreambabybar.com**

During the week, this low-lit cocktail bar is a laid-back spot for a
nice-but-not-too-fancy catch-up with friends. Then, come the
weekend, when the sun finally sets, Dream Baby takes on another
life, with every available square foot transformed into a de facto
dance floor. The music is a constant stream of throwback tracks,

Try it!
LEARN TO TANGO

Forget the bump and grind. Impress your
other half with tango lessons for beginners
at The Tango Company, in Midtown. You'll
feel like you're a pro on *Dancing with the
Stars* in no time (*www.tangoclassesnyc.com*).

ranging from 60s classics to the 90s boy-band crowd pleasers – all prime for singing along to until 4am when the lights are turned up. What more could you want for a night out?

SOLAS

Map 2; 232 East 9th Street, East Village; ///speak.drain.matter; 212-375-0297

Catering to a rowdy crowd of 20-somethings, this bi-level bar churns out a popping top-40 playlist for crazy weekend dance parties. It's an unexpected transformation; earlier in the evening Solas looks like your average run-down Irish pub, with happy hour specials stuck in the window. As the night wears on, lines of hopefuls snake out the door and the multiroom venue gets packed with partygoers ready to dance with friends.

BEMBE

Map 4; 81 South 6th Street, Williamsburg, Brooklyn; ///chimp.ally.candle; www.bembe.us

The buzz from this little dance hall is so palpable that it radiates down the street. DJs play an up-tempo mix of Caribbean, Latin, and Afrobeats, which are often joined by live percussionists (who might even let you have a go on their drums). The crowd is friendly and pretty relaxed thanks to the bar's potent rum punch. We challenge you not to stay until closing.

» **Don't leave without** sipping a Caipirinha. It's sharp, refreshing, and the perfect accompaniment to the music.

FRIENDS & LOVERS

Map 5; 641 Classon Avenue, Crown Heights, Brooklyn;
///comical.cared.sides; www.fnlbk.com

Friends and lovers make their way to Friends & Lovers for the mother of nights out. A skip and a jump away from a car repair shop, the incongruous club throws awesome theme nights where house DJs get the party jumping to funk, soul, and electro grooves.
» Don't leave without making your way to the Future Old School all-rap dance party, on the last Saturday of the month. Expect classic, addictive rap – the route to any and every 20-something's heart.

NOWADAYS

Map 6; 56-06 Cooper Avenue, Ridgewood, Queens; ///pipe.scarcely.slug;
www.nowadays.nyc

Industrial chic and irresistible DJ beats mean Nowadays gives off all the vibes of a Berlin nightclub. With its big outdoor area (finally, NYC, more please!), this Queens outpost is the perfect place for summer party nights that continue on to mimosas in the morning.

SHRINE

Map 6; 2271 Adam Clayton Powell Jr. Boulevard, Harlem;
///giving.shared.lung; www.shrinenyc.com

Early evening is dinner time at Shrine, with locals bopping along to live music as they chow down on burgers and chicken wings. But as midnight approaches, the place transforms into a late-night party. Diners get tipsy on mango mojitos, and cool kids turn up to dance to

It's really worth coming for dinner and staying put. You'll avoid the line, and experience the change of vibe.

the beats of DJs from Japan, Nigeria, Jamaica, and Senegal, often with a brass accompaniment. It's a hot-spot for fun-filled carnival-style nights.

HOME SWEET HOME

Map 2; 131 Chrystie Street # 1, Lower East Side;
///privately.decreased.harsh; www.homesweethomethebar.com

Disco ball? Check. Eclectic playlist? Check. Taxidermy? Er, check. Home Sweet Home has got it all. This popular Lower East Side dive bar-turned-club is a staple with a young, energetic, and eccentric crowd who love to dance and sweat profusely into the wee hours of the night. If you go in with the right attitude – in other words, ready to dance – you'll be sure to leave with a new group of friends, who'll want to grab a dollar slice with you at 3am and continue the festivities elsewhere.

BLACK FLAMINGO

Map 4; 168 Borinquen Place, Williamsburg, Brooklyn;
///super.locate.stacks; www.blackflamingonyc.com

Come Friday, young professionals log off for the day, rendezvous with their friends, and make their way to cooler-than-cool Black Flamingo. As the night ticks on, this plant-based and Miami-inspired taqueria, plonked opposite a school playground, transforms into a club. And beneath the cork-tile ceiling, the city's best house and techno DJs set up shop to entertain the masses.

LGBTQ+ Scene

The city that arguably sparked the LGBTQ+ Rights Movement is still at it. You'll discover a glorious and ever-changing host of queer venues, drag shows, and nightclubs alongside some time-tested favorites.

GOOD ROOM

Map 4; 98 Meserole Avenue, Greenpoint, Brooklyn; ///party.powder.patio; www.goodroombk.com

This Brooklyn party house has a few rooms, each as hedonistic as the next. Other electronic-focused nightclubs might have fallen by the wayside but the Good Room is going strong, with DJs and performers keeping LGBTQ+ elders and their allies partying.

» Don't leave without swinging by the Bad Room in the back, which usually has a steam machine going.

HOUSE OF YES

Map 4; 2 Wyckoff Avenue, Bushwick, Brooklyn; ///broker.puzzle.fans; www.houseofyes.org

House of Yes is known by locals for being an extremely inclusive establishment, and a lynchpin of the LGBTQ+ community. It's such a star that it's put Wyckoff Avenue on the map, with more businesses popping up along this thoroughfare. Fans love the performance venue and club's themed nights – where costume is an absolute must – and its outlandish performances. We're talking drag, carnival, burlesque, circus, and oh so much more.

CUBBYHOLE

Map 1; 281 West 12th Street, West Village; ///chimp.shades.coherent; 212-243-9041

Despite New York's thriving LGBTQ+ scene, Cubbyhole is one of the only lesbian bars in the city. The space itself is diminutive and divey, with an overzealous mash-up of ceiling decorations and paper lanterns that make the bar feel even smaller. And yet, this corner hangout is a vital part of the queer community, its welcoming atmosphere a haven for all visitors, whatever their story. Bonus: margaritas are only $3 on Tuesdays.

This place flies under the radar but it deserves way more attention. The Lesbian Herstory Archives, in Brooklyn, was founded in 1970 to record often-overlooked lesbian history (*www.lesbianherstoryarchives. org*). A passionate group of women run the center and throw cultured evening events for the discerning queer woman, along with her friends and allies. Expect stirring speakers and author events, plus glasses of wine and the most welcoming people in the city.

HARDWARE

Map 3; 697 Tenth Avenue, Hell's Kitchen; ///flood.origins.tiles;
www.hardware-bar.com

Brought to you by the owners of Playhouse, in the West Village, this is one of Manhattan's finest LGBTQ+ bars. Duct tape and pliers once lined the shelves of this former hardware store, but today this bustling Hell's Kitchen venue houses some of the city's best drag shows every night of the week. Performers are energetic, tucks are tight, and the crowd of revelers are joyfully living their best lives.

METROPOLITAN

Map 4; 559 Lorimer Street, Williamsburg, Brooklyn; ///swing.older.debit;
www.metropolitanbarny.com

It's all about feeling at home in this cozy Billyburg bar. Whether you're gay, bi, straight, trans, questioning – whatever – there's a chair ready and waiting for you. Not forgetting a nice outdoor patio, pool table, comfy couches, DJ sets, and even a couple of fireplaces that are lit in winter (the decor is inspired by a 1950s ski lodge plucked from a glossy catalogue). It's a welcoming home away from home.

PLAYHOUSE

Map 1; 100A Seventh Avenue, West Village; ///driver.script.chip;
www.playhousebar.com

A stone's throw from the site of the historic Stonewall riots of 1969, this West Village bar is a more-toned down version of its Hell's Kitchen iteration, Hardware. Still, enter through the doors of what was once a theater box office and stumble down the stairwell, like Alice entering Wonderland, and you'll be greeted by fabulous drag and music performances. It might be new to the Village, having opened in 2019, but Playhouse is here to stay.

3 DOLLAR BILL

Map 4; 260 Meserole Street, Bushwick, Brooklyn;
///surely.hype.aside; www.3dollarbillbk.com

Inclusivity across every spectrum is the order du jour at Brooklyn's premier queer performance venue, with the bar acting as a hub for anyone who may not feel welcome elsewhere. Run by Irish-born and immensely house-proud Brenda, who you might see pottering about the place with a broom, this Americana bar and venue hosts drag shows and themed costume nights. Looking for a more low-key night with the locals? 3 Dollar Bill also puts on TV watching parties and flea markets.

» Don't leave without heading to Sutherland, the warehouse space at the back of the bar, for an all-night dance party.

Try it!
BURLESQUE

Always fantasized about twirling tassels like Dita Von Teese? The School of Burlesque in Noho runs weekend classes – perfect for brushing up ahead of an underground ball (*www.schoolofburlesque.com*).

An entertaining evening in
Greenwich Village

Greenwich Village has long been a late-night entertainment hub, and with NYU's campus buildings scattered throughout the neighborhood, bright-eyed students continue to fuel this area's dynamic spirit. Walking down MacDougal Street is an assault on the senses, the aromas of Indian, Vietnamese, Mexican, and Ethiopian cuisine all vying for your attention, as hawkers bark out offers for basement comedy shows. As the sun sets, revelers pack into historic bars and quirky new venues, ready for lots of laughs (and drinks).

1. Baker & Co
259 Bleecker Street,
Greenwich Village;
www.bakernco.com
///flip.proud.sing

2. Saigon Shack
114 MacDougal Street,
Greenwich Village;
www.saigonshack.com
///sector.festivity.held

3. Comedy Cellar
117 MacDougal Street,
Greenwich Village;
www.comedycellar.com
//groups.sugar.fumes

4. Kettle of Fish
59 Christopher Street,
Greenwich Village;
www.kettleoffishnyc.com
///clues.slave.stores

📍 **Washington Square Park** ///popped.ahead.drum

📍 **Stonewall Inn** ///cheese.chop.bronze

WEST VILLAGE

STREET

HUDSON STREET

GROVE STREET

MORTON STREET

Have a nightcap at KETTLE OF FISH

This friendly sports bar, once frequented by Jack Kerouac and Bob Dylan, is the ideal spot for a nightcap.

WEST 10TH STREET

VILLAGE SQUARE

The historic **Stonewall Inn**, *site of the 1969 Stonewall riots, is still a bastion of New York's LGBTQ+ community.*

CHRISTOPHER STREET

SHERIDAN SQUARE

WEST 8TH STREET

4

GROVE STREET

WEST 4TH STREET

GREENWICH VILLAGE

6TH AVENUE

7TH AVENUE SOUTH

Washington Square Park *has long been a gathering spot for locals and street performers, who keep the park lively well into the evening.*

Nurse a drink at BAKER & CO

The happy-hour drinks at this friendly Italian restaurant are best enjoyed on the breezy patio.

WEST 4TH STREET

Washington Square Park

1

BLEECKER STREET

WEST 3RD STREET

FATHER DEMO SQUARE

Fill up at SAIGON SHACK

Follow the students to this casual spot for a steaming bowl of Vietnamese pho.

BEDFORD STREET

BLEECKER STREET

6TH AVENUE

MACDOUGAL STREET

3

Enjoy a show at COMEDY CELLAR

Get ready to laugh until you cry at NYC's premiere comedy club, where famous faces like Amy Schumer and Aziz Ansari regularly drop by.

2

0 meters	100
0 yards	100

OUTDOORS

You need only look at the traffic-clogged streets to see that life in NYC is hectic. Urban farms, vast parks, and scenic riversides offer the calm and freedom locals cherish.

Green Spaces

New York's parks aren't just open spaces.
They're gathering spots, birthday venues, date
locales, and much-needed respites from the city's
grid of steel, brick, and concrete.

WASHINGTON SQUARE PARK

Map 1; entrance via Washington Square North, Greenwich Village;
///points.stands.waddle

Washington Square Park feels like the center of the universe. NYU students discuss politics on the lawns, colleagues rendezvous for alfresco meetings, buskers play peppy tunes, and old timers people-watch from the benches. The park buzzes with a palpable energy that can only be expected from the heart of the world's most famous city.

PROSPECT PARK

Map 5; entrance via West Drive, Bartel-Pritchard Square, Park Slope,
Brooklyn; ///faded.pipes.solved; www.prospectpark.org

Upon its completion in the 19th century, Prospect Park was visited by Brooklynites wanting to practice their archery and play croquet on summer weekends, and ice skate on the lake in winter. Fast forward to today and the scene hasn't much changed. Okay, ice skating isn't allowed, nor archery, but you get the idea. The summer sees cool kids Rollerblade the park's paths, and families enjoy picnics. Come winter, and friends cuddle up for the park's seasonal concerts and, when it snows, hold huge snowball fights. And, whatever the season, every morning there seem to be more dogs than people on the Great Lawn.

» Don't leave without practicing your vinyāsa flow at a class with Park Slope yoga studio Bend + Bloom in summer.

THE HIGH LINE
Map 1; entrance via 30th Street and 11th Avenue, Hudson Yards; ///wipe.spray.goods; www.thehighline.org

Nowhere better symbolizes New York's ingenuity than the High Line. On what was once an elevated train track set for demolition, the urban park winds around graffiti-sprayed apartment blocks — each twist and turn offering a new view and patch of flora. It's no surprise that locals often commute through the park, an obligatory coffee in hand; less tooting traffic, more pleasant scenery.

THE BATTERY
Map 5; entrance via Battery Place and State Street, Financial District; ///stacks.sooner.scary; www.thebattery.org

A hot contender for New York's loveliest picnic spot, the Battery offers stunning, sparkling views of the Hudson and Lady Liberty. Once a military stronghold, the park is now popular with office workers doing their daily workouts and out-of-towners drinking in that view.

CENTRAL PARK

Map 3; entrance via Park Road, Grand Army Plaza, Upper East Side;
///seated.trails.trades; www.centralparknyc.org

The green lungs of the city, the people's park, the star of the movies. New Yorkers are rightly proud of this, their backyard. This is where parents teach their kids to ride a bike, nervous lovers pop the question, and friends toast birthdays. And with community dance sessions, musical shows, and fun runs galore, it's no wonder Central Park is every local's favorite green space.

» Don't leave without visiting the Hallett Nature Sanctuary; the woodland is so peaceful and you'll have the best city views all to yourself.

BRYANT PARK

Map 3; entrance via Sixth Avenue and West 42nd Street, Midtown;
///turned.bunk.guilty; www.bryantpark.org

Tucked behind New York Public Library is lovely Bryant Park, where freelancers take advantage of the park's free wifi and numerous tables. Sure, the park is small but the events program is extensive, from outdoor movie nights in summer to Winter Village in, well, winter.

VAN CORTLANDT PARK

Map 6; entrance via Van Cortlandt Park South, Kingsbridge, The Bronx;
///quarrel.rice.social; 718-430-1890

As joggers pant around the perimeter of Van Cortlandt Park, and budding baseball stars practice their swing, families and friends set up camp for a relaxed day of sun-soaking; they sprawl across the park's

The 1 train journey to the park is worth it in itself; it's above ground from 125th Street, and the views are amazing.

vast lawn and devour their bountiful picnics. When dusk arrives, beers and portable speakers are produced for an alfresco night of socializing.

BROOKLYN BRIDGE PARK

**Map 5; entrance via New Dock Street, Fulton Ferry District, Brooklyn;
///detect.oldest.melon; www.brooklynbridgepark.org**

Across the East River from the soul-soaring Manhattan skyline, Brooklyn Bridge Park has it all. Thinking of a bike ride? No problem, there's a great cycle path. Fancy skimming rocks? Join local parents teaching their kids on Pebble Beach. Want to sunbathe? There's lots of space in front of Empire Stores. All with those mesmerizing views that lucky Brooklynites get to see every day.

ST. NICHOLAS PARK

**Map 6; entrance via St. Nicholas Avenue, Harlem; ///robots.behave.daily;
www.stnicholasparknyc.org**

If you want Manhattan's best parks, continue uptown. St. Nick's might seem an unassuming backyard for City College, but it's home to stately Hamilton Grange, the former home of Broadway muse Alexander Hamilton. These days the park belongs to the people of Harlem and the sense of community is evident. Volunteers pitch in for garden cleanups, students congregate between classes on the park's never-ending sea of basketball courts, and dog-walkers chitchat during the dog run.

On the Water

In a city of skyscrapers, it's easy to forget that New York is actually surrounded by water – and lots of it. Locals love making the most of it, too, even if it's just escaping the city by walking the water's promenades.

ROLLERBLADE ALONG BROOKLYN BRIDGE PARK

Map 5; start at Pier 1, Brooklyn Bridge Park, Fulton Ferry District, Brooklyn; ///lights.jump.farms

Make like it's the 90s and don your Rollerblades. Brooklyn Bridge Park has riverside esplanades to coast along – the perfect way to cool off on a hot day. You'll probably be passed by dexterous kids but there's nothing at stake besides your dignity. If you fancy something a little more contained, there's a roller rink on Pier 2.

CANOE THE GOWANUS CANAL

Map 5 ; start at 165 2nd Street, Gowanus, Brooklyn; ///pits.desk.boat; www.gowanuscanal.org

Like most New York bodies of water, Brooklyn's Gowanus Canal has faced years of neglect and pollution. Enter: the Gowanus Dredgers Canoe Club, a local nonprofit that aims to revitalize the canal. The heroic society organizes donation-based outings on the water, where canoeists learn about conservation efforts while cruising the waterway. What your trip lacks in crystal-clear water it makes up for in history, as conveyed by infectiously passionate guides.

» **Don't leave without** having a mooch around nearby Red Hook, a charming waterfront stretch that feels more like a quaint fishing town than part of the big city.

WALK THE EAST RIVER PROMENADE

Map 5; start at Pier 42, Lower East Side; ///active.boats.flat

Even New Yorkers forget about East River Park. It's an almost utopian swath of the city, where everyone has a healthy glow. This is by and large thanks to a well-kept track and tennis courts, which draw fitness fanatics, but it's the never-ending waterside promenade that's the park's star player. It's a peaceful place to walk along the river and drink in the gorgeous views of the Williamsburg Bridge.

RIDE THE STATEN ISLAND FERRY

Map 5; start at Whitehall Terminal, Financial District;
///allows.gender.resist; www.siferry.com

To really bliss out on the water, head across the Hudson to NYC's least populated borough. Staten Island locals are ferried to and from work on this free ferry during rush hour, scrolling through their social media nonplussed while the Statue of Liberty and Ellis Island rumble past. But, for the rest of the day, the 25-minute ride is the domain of everyone else, all gasping and pointing at the ferry's unbeatable views.

Solo, Pair, Crowd

We all need a gulp of salty sea (or river) air. And, handily, NYC has a number of watery adventures for just that.

FLYING SOLO
Swat up on maritime history
Red Hook's Waterfront Barge Museum, based on a restored 1914 boat, is tiny. Learn about maritime history with Captain David, a former cruise-ship juggler who now lives aboard the barge. He'll have loads of local recommendations for you, too.

IN A PAIR
Salsa beside the water
Grab a partner and move your hips to the beat at Williamsburg's Domino Park, which hosts weekly salsa sessions and free classes in the fall. Overlooking the East River, the park's views are incredible.

IN A CROWD
Pedal on the Hudson
The BYO NYC Cycleboat takes pedal boarding up a notch, with 12 seats for you and your friends to cycle your way from New Jersey to Manhattan.

KAYAK THE EAST RIVER

**Map 5; start at Brooklyn Bridge Boathouse, Pier 2, Brooklyn Bridge Park,
Fulton Ferry District, Brooklyn; ///dared.vibes.them;
www.brooklynbridgepark.org**

Sure, watching Manhattan drift into the distance aboard the
Staten Island Ferry is thrilling. But what about paddling the waters
that bound the city for yourself? During the summer months you
can use a kayak from the Brooklyn Bridge Park Boathouse for free
and glide along the East River. Your 20-minute time slot comes not
only with a weathered kayak and life vest, but also a crew of lovely
volunteers doling out paddling instructions, plus those incredible
views of Manhattan along the way.

» Don't leave without slurping down oysters and a cocktail at PILOT,
the floating oyster bar at Pier 6.

RELAX ON BRIGHTON BEACH

**Map 6; start at Riegelmann Boardwalk, Brighton Beach, Brooklyn;
///twin.memo.vivid**

Out on Brooklyn's southernmost tip is Brighton Beach, an invitingly
named neighborhood. Home to Russian and Eastern and Central
European communities, this outpost is fronted by a lovely sandy
beach – the perfect spot for a bit of R & R. Stroll around the
Riegelmann Boardwalk before joining locals stretched out on the
sand, or people-watch cliques talking animatedly to one another in
their native tongues. While away an afternoon here before heading
a few steps inland for an array of affordable restaurants serving fare
from the motherland (think smoked fish washed down with vodka).

Community Gardens and Urban Farms

Within the concrete cityscape, gardens and urban farms have become vital spaces for residents to connect with nature, and each other. There are plenty to visit – here are just a handful.

THE BATTERY URBAN FARM

Map 5; The Battery, State Street and Battery Place, Financial District; ///stores.gossip.loves; www.thebattery.org

Plopped in Lower Manhattan's Battery *(p169)* is this lovely plot, which was created to teach New Yorkers all about sustainable farming. On any given day, you'll find green-fingered volunteers and local school groups harvesting veg that will go on to be donated to local organizations. It's a little bit of respite from the city's hectic Financial District.

LA FINCA DEL SUR

Map 6; 110 East 138th Street, Mott Haven, The Bronx; ///rainy.bids.flips

Founded by a group of local women, this garden and farm is a haven in the concrete expanse of the South Bronx; volunteers chat and laugh and work on the plant beds, unperturbed by the trains that rush past. The nonprofit prides itself on empowering women of color, as well as growing food for its gardeners. Support the cause by buying La Finca del Sur's produce at the South Bronx Farmers' Market.

ELIZABETH STREET GARDEN

Map 1; Elizabeth Street (between Prince and Spring), Nolita; ///birds.paying.less; www.elizabethstreetgarden.com

Community space meets sculpture garden at Elizabeth Street. Picture this: statues of lions and Greek goddesses dotted between flower beds, old-timer Italians chatting on their daily garden stroll, office workers joyfully escaping their screens for a much-needed slice of nature, and couples meeting for alfresco dates. It might be facing the ongoing threat of demolition, but that's not stopping Manhattanites from enjoying this nonprofit garden – if anything, it's making them visit more.

6TH STREET AND AVENUE B COMMUNITY GARDEN

Map 2; Corner of 6th Street and Avenue B, Alphabet City; ///teach.cared.riots; www.newsite.6bgarden.org

A social enterprise since 1983, Alphabet City's community garden is a tranquil refuge, open on weekends from April through October. Join locals sitting on the garden's benches, quietly chatting, reading, and listening to the birdsong that rings out from the plot's winged friends. The garden also hosts enchanting music and poetry events.

>> Don't leave without stopping by the delightful Creative Little Garden and 6BC Botanical Garden, both of which are also on 6th Street.

GOVERNORS ISLAND
TEACHING GARDEN

Map 5; 778 Enright Road, Governors Island; ///claims.video.dare;
212-788-7900

Hop on a ferry to the serene and car-free Governors Island for a proper gulp of fresh air. Sure, the island's urban farm is overrun with kids on field trips during the week but come the weekend and it's all yours. Learn all about the eco-friendly garden, take a class to hone in on a specific topic, or just befriend the farm's gaggle of goats.

LIZ CHRISTY COMMUNITY GARDEN

Map 2; East Houston Street (between 2nd Avenue and Bowery),
Lower East Side; ///shop.skill.port; www.lizchristygarden.us

Size isn't everything, you know. Take this small garden, which is thought as city's first community garden. In the 1970s, New York resident Liz Christy and a group of "Green Guerillas" banded together to clean up and revitalize a vacant lot with herbaceous plants and wildflowers. Today, dedicated volunteers carry on the good work so New Yorkers can continue to enjoy the lovely little space.

BROOKLYN GRANGE ROOFTOP FARM

Map 6; 37–18 Northern Boulevard, Long Island City, Queens;
///handed.renew.ridge; www.brooklyngrangefarm.com

What do a chicken coop, rows of veggies, and a seasonal market have in common? They're all hidden on top of an ordinary office building in Queens. Brooklyn Grange actually has a collection of impressive urban farms peppered across the city, all of which are adored by local sustainability warriors. Head over to the Queens rooftop for the Saturday Open House to stock up on some homegrown produce, have a go at seeding some plant babies, and take in the Manhattan skyline.

» **Don't leave without** buying a bottle of the hot sauce, made with peppers and herbs grown on the rooftop garden.

HARLEM GROWN
Map 6; 118 West 134th Street, Harlem; ///bench.unity.flags; www.harlemgrown.org

This Harlem-based nonprofit is so much more than just an urban farm – the big-hearted organization also mentors local youths about nutrition, sustainable food, and the environment with hands-on education. This is possible thanks to Harlem Grown's army of passionate volunteers who all pitch in with nurturing both the plants and the children across 12 urban agriculture facilities, including farms, greenhouses, and school gardens.

Try it!
BECOME A GARDENER

Stop by Harlem Grown on Saturday mornings for a half-day of garden volunteering (11am–3pm). Gardening experience isn't necessary but be prepared to get your hands dirty.

Streets and Alleys

New York City moves at a brisk pace but there are some seriously idyllic alleys that deserve more of a leisurely meander. Forget your itinerary and make like a flâneur on these enchanting streets.

GROVE STREET

Map 1; Grove Street, West Village; ///post.medium.leap

This adorable street is quintessential West Village: winding and narrow, lined with gorgeous townhouses and cozy restaurants, and populated with effortlessly cool New Yorkers. But its main claim to fame? It's home to Monica's apartment in *Friends*, of course. Once you've got a few pictures, continue down the street to Grove Court. The quiet courtyard, home to handsome houses from the 1850s, feels light-years away from the thrum of the city.

WILLIAMSBURG BRIDGE

Map 5; Williamsburg Bridge, Williamsburg, Brooklyn; ///fades.tickets.plants

Meet Brooklyn Bridge's younger sister, the Williamsburg Bridge. Okay, we know it's not a street, nor an alley, but we couldn't exclude it. Connecting the Lower East Side and Williamsburg, the bridge is always alive with the hurried footsteps of commuters walking or jogging to work but – unlike Brooklyn Bridge – it never seems to attract crushing crowds waving selfie sticks. This means you can enjoy the bridge's beautiful engineering and East River views in relative peace. That being said, beware of the rumbling JMZ trains, which speed by at a deafening clip.

MACDOUGAL ALLEY

Map 1; MacDougal Alley, Greenwich Village; ///glee.hired.stow

It's like this charming alley has been plucked from the pages of an novel, with its cobblestones and cute brick cottages, and plonked in the heart of the city. This mews became an enclave for artists in the early 20th century, when Gertrude Vanderbilt Whitney welcomed "lesser-known" artists into her studio (Edward Hopper and Thomas Hart Benton among them) before she founded a little museum called The Whitney (p119). Want to learn more? Join one of the tours run by the New York Studio School.

» Don't leave without strolling south down MacDougal Street, just off the alley, which is the heart of Greenwich Village.

Look for the sign bearing a rooster that hangs above a gate between Broadway and West End Avenue. Beyond, you'll find Pomander Walk, a whimsical, British-looking street of cute houses inspired by a play of the same name.

JORALEMON STREET

Map 5; Joralemon Street, Brooklyn Heights, Brooklyn;
///pushes.brick.crazy

Brooklyn Heights is surely one of the most serene neighborhoods in NYC and Joralemon Street is particularly picture-perfect. Rows of well-maintained brownstones line the streets, their brick facades alternating in a rainbow of colors. The idyllic scene is bolstered by plentiful greenery and flowers potted in street signs, little details that make the street feel like a movie set. Walk east to 129 Joralemon, a "Queen Anne"-style landmarked mansion-turned-apartment that dates from the 1890s (and has some pretty creepy Gothic touches).

» Don't leave without getting a photo of the delightfully colorful homes found at the crossroads of Joralemon and Columbia Place: the townhouses here are arranged in a red-blue-green-white pattern.

STRIVER'S ROW

Map 6; 530 East 6th Street, Harlem; ///funded.line.levels;
www.striversrownyc.org

The striking brownstones of Striver's Row tell a story of economic mobility in America. These row houses were built way back in 1895 and intended for well-to-do white New Yorkers, but an economic depression meant potential buyers left the city to rebuild their fortunes elsewhere. Harlem, meanwhile, saw its Black community grow and, in the 1920s, the buildings were finally made available to Black New Yorkers. The gorgeous brownstones attracted a wave of young aspirants – or "strivers" – who are famous for the Harlem Renaissance. Today the gorgeous houses on Striver's Row are

Pop around the corner to Make My Cake for a Southern-inspired slice from Harlem matriarch "Ma Smith." property gold, and the street is lovely to walk along. Plus, very few travelers venture this far north so you'll have the place all to yourself.

ELIZABETH STREET

Map 1; Elizabeth Street, Nolita; ///lofts.exam.chemistry

Like countless New York City streets, Elizabeth sits at the crossroads between two distinct neighborhoods, its personality morphing as you cross the divide. Start at Houston, where this quaint strip is arguably Nolita's most picturesque shopping street, known for its upscale boutiques and chic clientele – this is the place for window shopping. Once you cross Kenmare, you'll be greeted by the comforting smell of noodles and frothy puffs of smoke drifting from Chinatown's hole-in-the-wall dim sum shops.

NINTH AVENUE

Map 1; Ninth Avenue, Meatpacking District; ///label.richer.rocky

Named for its industrial past as a slaughterhouse hub, the Meatpacking District is now a high-fashion neighborhood with a likewise cooler-than-cool cohort of locals. This is best seen on Ninth Avenue, where fashionistas and that-model-you-know-from-TV can be spotted clip-clopping down the street. It feels like a vestige of old New York, especially if you carry on to Gansevoort Street, with its cobblestones. This is also a great place to start the High Line (p169), where the magic continues above street level.

Nearby Getaways

Of course New Yorkers love their city but sometimes a change of scene is just what's needed. Fortunately, the Big Apple has various tempting day trips right on its doorstep.

HOBOKEN

30-minute bus ride from Port Authority Midtown Bus Terminal

A hop, skip, and a jump (and a bus journey) away across the Hudson, in New Jersey, is this cobblestone-clad city. Young professionals make a beeline for Hoboken on their days off, drawn to its stellar restaurants and bars that lack the intensity of NYC. It might be a city, but Hoboken is pure charm with its low-slung redbrick buildings, pavement cafés, and pretty waterfront. It also affords some incredible views of Manhattan, especially from Sinatra Park, which is named after Hoboken-born crooner Frank.

» Don't leave without buying a latte at Bwè Kafe, a family-run café that supports Love for Haiti, a nonprofit for Haitian youth.

SANDY HOOK

30-minute ferry ride from East 35th Street Pier

Sandy beaches dotted with sun-soakers, clear lapping waters speckled with fish, and circling seagulls overhead; for a proper beach escape, Sandy Hook, in New Jersey, ticks all the boxes. There are a variety of beaches to choose from, like clothing-optional Gunnison, a popular spot with adults looking to let go, literally, plus plenty of opportunities for kayaking and cycling, if you'd rather ditch the beach towel for something more exertive.

TARRYTOWN

1 hour train ride from Grand Central Terminal; www.tarrytowngov.com

Tarrytown has become a hot spot for goths and lovers of the macabre, which isn't surprising. After all, this was the setting of *Sleepy Hollow*, thanks to its undeniably creepy stately houses, including the Gothic Revival Lyndhurst Mansion. And locals really live up to their hometown's reputation, decorating their homes for Halloween with theatrical flourishes. If you're more about pints than frights, there are some really cute bars here, plus a couple of wineries outside of the town.

THE ROCKAWAYS

1.5-hour subway ride from Pennsylvania Station

The town of Rockaways, in Queens, and its string of beaches are fast becoming the go-to coastal hot spot for hipsters who need a quick flop and drop. And for a thrifty $2.75 subway ride, who can blame them? There's the boardwalk to saunter down, chicken poppers and beer to be devoured just a stone's throw from the beach, and the bastion of LGBTQ+ fun, Jacob Riis Park, to explore. Oh, and miles of glorious, golden sand, of course.

PRINCETON

1.5-hour drive from Downtown; www.princetonnj.gov

Picture this: collegiate Gothic buildings and expanses of well-manicured greenery, peppered with students clutching books and cycling to lectures. Welcome to Princeton, one of America's most prestigious and old-school universities. This is the day trip New Yorkers roll out when they want to feel a bit more intellectual – an exploration of the Princeton Battlefield with the in-laws or lunch in civilized Palmer Square with the girls. Princeton's charisma never disappoints.

BEACON

1.5-hour train ride from Grand Central Terminal

Due north from NYC, the cute town of Beacon is the go-to place to get some fresh ideas for your apartment. Make for Storm King Art Center, a 30-minute shuttle from the town's center, for arty inspiration. It's an open-air sculpture museum and the artworks are so striking against the backdrop of the New York county countryside. Once you've had your fill of art, head back to Beacon's cute Main Street, lined with 19th-century buildings housing vintage stores and artisan boutiques galore, to buy something in miniature.

» Don't leave without visiting Dia:Beacon, a world-class contemporary art museum that's housed in a former Nabisco box-printing factory.

HARRIMAN STATE PARK

1.5-hour train ride from Penn Station; www.parks.ny.gov

We know, the city can be a lot to handle, especially if you've arrived from somewhere with a slower pace and more outdoor space. Luckily, public transportation makes it very simple to get away; a short while after departing Penn Station, you can join the Ramapo-Dunderberg trail, which passes through Harriman State Park. New York parents, their kids and own parents in tow, love hiking the park's stunning landscape, stopping to enjoy its vast lakes and point out birdlife. Sound good? You can also stay at a lean-to or camp out in the park – perfect for s'mores and a campfire singalong.

Try it!
BIRD-WATCHING

Life is manic, isn't it? We suggest bird-watching to switch off. Download the iBird Pro Birding App and head off early to Harriman State Park. We swear the birdsong alone will bring you inner peace.

A perfect day out on the
Upper West Side

Come the weekend, locals flock to this leafy stretch of NYC for some much needed R&R. Here, within the depths of Manhatten's concrete jungle, you'll find the vast fresh air pocket of Central Park. Built for the public in the 19th century, this is, and has always been, the people's backyard – a green gathering spot for New Yorkers across the city. Before reaching the park, wander through the pretty brownstone-laden streets to the west – once home to John Lennon and Leonard Bernstein – and take a gulp of fresh air at Riverside Park.

1. Lolo's Seafood Shack
303 West 116th Street,
Harlem; www.lolosseafood
shack.com
///late.bunny.shock

2. Riverside Park
Upper West Side
www.nycgovparks.org
///letter.taker.piles

3. Gorgeous Brownstones
87th Street,
Upper West Side
///items.hype.likely

4. Met Roof Garden Bar
1000 Fifth Avenue,
Upper East Side;
www.metmuseum.org
///loose.pounds.violin

5. Paddleboating
East 72nd Street & Center
Drive, Central Park; www.the
centralparkboathouse.com
///beside.rift.much

**Jackie Kennedy Onassis
Reservoir**
///learn.divisions.broom

Hudson River

HENRY HUDSON PARKWAY

WEST 57TH ST

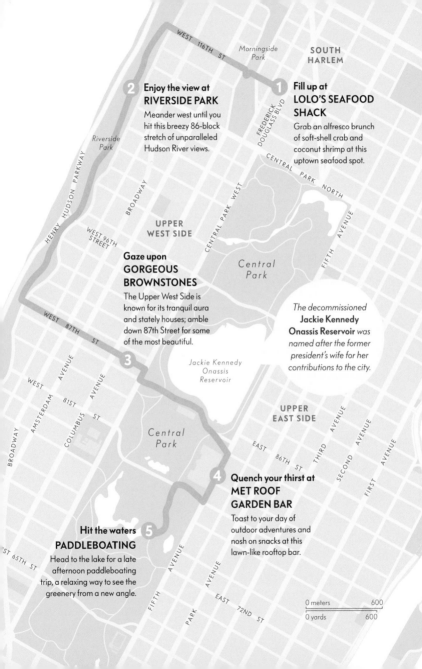

2 Enjoy the view at
RIVERSIDE PARK

Meander west until you
hit this breezy 86-block
stretch of unparalleled
Hudson River views.

1 Fill up at
**LOLO'S SEAFOOD
SHACK**

Grab an alfresco brunch
of soft-shell crab and
coconut shrimp at this
uptown seafood spot.

**UPPER
WEST SIDE**

Gaze upon
**GORGEOUS
BROWNSTONES**

The Upper West Side is
known for its tranquil aura
and stately houses; amble
down 87th Street for some
of the most beautiful.

The decommissioned
**Jackie Kennedy
Onassis Reservoir** *was
named after the former
president's wife for her
contributions to the city.*

**UPPER
EAST SIDE**

4 Quench your thirst at
**MET ROOF
GARDEN BAR**

Toast to your day of
outdoor adventures and
nosh on snacks at this
lawn-like rooftop bar.

Hit the waters
PADDLEBOATING **5**

Head to the lake for a late
afternoon paddleboating
trip, a relaxing way to see the
greenery from a new angle.

*SOUTH
HARLEM*

*Morningside
Park*

*Riverside
Park*

*Central
Park*

*Jackie Kennedy
Onassis
Reservoir*

*Central
Park*

WEST 116TH ST

FREDERICK DOUGLASS BLVD

CENTRAL PARK NORTH

CENTRAL PARK WEST

FIFTH AVENUE

BROADWAY

HENRY HUDSON PARKWAY

WEST 96TH STREET

WEST 87TH ST

WEST 81ST ST

AMSTERDAM AVENUE

COLUMBUS AVENUE

BROADWAY

WEST 65TH ST

EAST 86TH ST

THIRD AVENUE

SECOND AVENUE

FIRST AVENUE

FIFTH AVENUE

PARK AVENUE

EAST 72ND ST

| 0 meters | 600 |
| 0 yards | 600 |

With a little research and preparation, this city will feel like a home away from home. Check out these websites to ensure a healthy, safe stay in New York City.

New York City
DIRECTORY

SAFE SPACES

New York City is diverse and inclusive, but should you feel uneasy at any point or want to find your community, there are spaces catering to different genders, sexualities, demographics, and religions.

www.92y.org
An inclusive Jewish-based cultural and community center.

www.alp.org
The Audre Lorde Project, a community organization for LGBTQ+ People of Color.

www.blackownedbrooklyn.com
A curated guide to Brooklyn's Black-owned businesses.

www.gaycenter.org
A space for New York City's LGBTQ+ community to meet and connect.

www.sixthstreetcenter.org
Community center and youth program space in the Alphabet City neighborhood.

HEALTH

Health care in America isn't free, so it's important to take out comprehensive health insurance for your visit. If you do need medical assistance, there are many pharmacies and hospitals across the city.

www.citymd.com
A list of nearby walk-in urgent care centers.

www.cvs.com
Pharmacy chain with locations all over the city, and a few open 24/7.

www.institute.org
An affordable community health center organization, featuring two free clinics for the uninsured.

www.nyp.org
New York-Presbyterian, a health care and hospital network with locations in the city.

www.plannedparenthood.org
Nonprofit organization providing sexual health care for all.

www.profiles.health.ny.gov
Resource detailing hospitals and their services throughout the state.

TRAVEL SAFETY ADVICE
Before you travel – and while you're here – always keep tabs on the latest regulations in New York City, and the US.

www.cdc.gov
National public health institute offering disease prevention and guidance.

www.coronavirus.health.ny.gov
COVID-19 news and advice from New York State.

www1.nyc.gov
New York Police Department website, including precinct news and information on how to report various crimes.

www.portal.311.nyc.gov
The city's official information hotline, with details on how to retrieve lost property.

www.safehorizon.org
Nonprofit helping survivors of domestic abuse, sexual assault, and other crimes.

www.travel.state.gov
Latest travel safety information.

ACCESSIBILITY
New York City is steadily becoming more accessible, with the goal of adding elevators to all subway stations by 2034. These resources will help make your journeys go smoothly.

www.new.mta.info/accessibility
List of accessible MTA stations and elevator and escalator status.

www.nycaccessible.com
Website and app with updates on subway station accessibility and outages.

www.nycgo.com
A list of accessible venues on the city's official tourism guide.

www1.nyc.gov
Resources to assist NYC's Deaf and Hard of Hearing community.

www.tdf.org
Nonprofit group increasing access to theaters for people with specific requirements.

ABOUT THE ILLUSTRATOR

Mantas Tumosa

*Creative designer and illustrator Mantas
moved from his home country of Lithuania
to London back in 2011. By day, he's busy
creating bold, minimalistic illustrations
that tell a story – such as the gorgeous
cover of this book. By night, he's dreaming
of adventures away, catching up on the
basketball, and cooking Italian food
(which he can't get enough of).*

Main Contributors Lauren Paley,
Bryan Pirolli, Kweku Ulzen

Senior Editor Lucy Richards

Senior Designer Tania Gomes

Project Editor Zoë Rutland

Project Art Editor Bharti Karakoti

Editors Elsepth Beidas,
Zoë Rutland, Lucy Sara-Kelly

Proofreader Kathryn Glendenning

Senior Cartographic Editor Casper Morris

Cartography Manager Suresh Kumar

Cartographer Ashif

Jacket Designer Tania Gomes

Jacket Illustrator Mantas Tumosa

Senior Production Editor Jason Little

Senior Production Controller Stephanie McConnell

Managing Editor Hollie Teague

Managing Art Editor Bess Daly

Art Director Maxine Pedliham

Publishing Director Georgina Dee

First edition 2021

Published in Great Britain by Dorling Kindersley Limited,
DK, One Embassy Gardens, 8 Viaduct Gardens,
London SW11 7BW.

The authorised representative in the EEA is
Dorling Kindersley Verlag GmbH. Arnulfstr. 124,
80636 Munich, Germany.

Published in the United States by DK Publishing,
1450 Broadway, Suite 801, New York, NY 10018.

Copyright © 2021 Dorling Kindersley Limited
A Penguin Random House Company
21 22 23 24 10 9 8 7 6 5 4 3 2

The publishers cannot accept responsibility for any consequences arising from
the use of this book, nor for any material on third party websites, and cannot
guarantee that any website address in this book will be a suitable source of
travel information.

A CIP catalog record for this book is available from the British Library.

A catalog record for this book is available from the Library of Congress.

ISSN: 1542 1554
ISBN: 978 0 2414 9067 9

Printed and bound in Canada.

www.dk.com

A NOTE FROM DK EYEWITNESS

The world is fast-changing and it's keeping us folk at
DK Eyewitness on our toes. We've worked hard to ensure
that this edition of New York City Like a Local is up-to-date
and reflects today's favourite places but we know that
standards shift, venues close, and new ones pop up in their
place. So, if you notice something has closed, we've got
something wrong or left something out, we want to hear
about it. Please drop us a line at travelguides@dk.com